More praise for

End This Depression Now!

"No book could be more timely. . . . Krugman pointedly reminds us that the economic and social costs of a premature pivot toward deficit reduction are catastrophic."

—*New York Review of Books*

"It's the sort of book you wish were compulsory reading, and want to quote to anyone who'll listen, because *End This Depression Now!* provides a comprehensive narrative of how we have ended up doing the opposite of what logic and history tell us we must do to get out of this crisis." —Decca Aitkenhead, *Guardian*

"[Krugman's] insistence on providing help for struggling American families is a welcome antidote to the Washington establishment's relentless focus on budget cuts." —*Foreign Policy*

"Paul Krugman breaks the mold with this practical answer to our increasingly troubled times from an economist who proves consistently right."

—Jon Snow, ITN

"Paul Krugman is stepping up to play the kind of role that John Maynard Keynes performed in the 1930s—arguing in clear accessible language for the government to spend to get us out of the slump."   —*Dissent*

"Keynes's vicar on earth. . . . His plea for immediate, universal demand expansion is unanswerable." —Simon Jenkins, *Guardian*

"Krugman's timely book summarizes how we reached this point, provides a scathing critique of austerity policies, and explains how to get people back to work."   —*Dollars & Sense*

"You might disagree with his thesis, but you'll keep on reading."   —*The Week*

"This book by the Nobel Prize winner is brilliantly timed."   —Andrew Hill, *Financial Times*

"Krugman is not afraid to take on anyone."   —*SF Weekly*

"[Krugman's] wit and bipartisanship ensure that this book will appeal to a broad swath of readers—from the Left to the Right, from the 99% to the 1%."   —*Publishers Weekly*

"An important contribution to the current study of economics and a reason for hope that effective solutions will be implemented again."   —*Kirkus Reviews*

PAUL KRUGMAN

END THIS DEPRESSION N☀W!

W. W. NORTON & COMPANY

NEW YORK LONDON

For information about permission to reproduce selections from this book,
write to Permissions, W. W. Norton & Company, Inc.,
500 Fifth Avenue, New York, NY 10110

For information about special discounts for bulk purchases, please contact
W. W. Norton Special Sales at specialsales@wwnorton.com or 800-233-4830

Manufacturing by Courier Westford
Production manager: Julia Druskin

Library of Congress Cataloging-in-Publication Data

Krugman, Paul R.
End this depression now! / Paul Krugman. — 1st ed.
p. cm.
Includes index.
ISBN 978-0-393-08877-9 (hardcover)
1. Financial crises—United States—History—21st century. 2. Recessions—
United States—History—21st century. 3. United States—Economic policy—
21st century. 4. Unemployment—United States—History—21st century.
I. Title.
HB3743.K78 2012
330.973—dc23

2012009067

ISBN 978-0-393-34508-7 pbk.

W. W. Norton & Company, Inc.
500 Fifth Avenue, New York, N.Y. 10110
www.wwnorton.com

W. W. Norton & Company Ltd.
Castle House, 75/76 Wells Street, London W1T 3QT

1 2 3 4 5 6 7 8 9 0

End
This Depression
Now!

Also by Paul Krugman

The Return of Depression Economics and the Crisis of 2008

The Conscience of a Liberal

Fuzzy Math

The Accidental Theorist

Pop Internationalism

Peddling Prosperity

The Age of Diminished Expectations

To the unemployed, who deserve better.

CONTENTS

PREFACE TO
THE PAPERBACK EDITION

I PUT THE HARDCOVER edition of *End This Depression Now!* to bed in February 2012, amid huge uncertainty about what the near future would hold. Who would win the U.S. election in November? Would financial crisis tear Europe apart? And how would the book's essential message hold up in the face of events?

Some of that uncertainty has now been resolved. In America, Democrats won a big but not complete election victory: they returned Barack Obama to the White House and expanded their Senate majority, but failed to overturn the Republican majority in the House of Representatives. In Europe, financial markets had calmed down to some extent, largely thanks to support from the European Central Bank, but the real economy continued to deteriorate for most of the continent. In particular, the already terrible situation in southern Europe grew even worse: both Greece and Spain now have higher unemployment than the United States had in the depths of the Great Depression. And during 2012 the euro zone as a whole slid back into recession.

Have any of these events changed the essential message of this book? The answer, unfortunately, is no; on the contrary, the message—that we are facing a vast, unnecessary catastrophe—is more relevant than ever. The advanced world remains in depression, with tens of millions of men and women seeking work but unable to find jobs, and with trillions of dollars' worth of economic potential going to waste. Yet the evidence is clearer than ever that this depression is gratuitous—that it is the result of nothing more fundamental than inadequate demand. And if governments would reverse their disastrous turn toward austerity and pursue renewed stimulus instead, we could have a rapid recovery.

Let's look at the current situation, and in particular at the prospects for action in America now that the U.S. election is behind us.

Europe's Austerity Disaster

If you want to understand where we are right now, the figure below is a good starting point. It shows unemployment rates in the United States and in the euro area, the group of mostly wealthy European nations that have adopted the euro as their common currency. It illustrates two key points: the two sides of the Atlantic shared a crisis from 2007 to 2010, but their situations have diverged since then.

Unemployment Rates

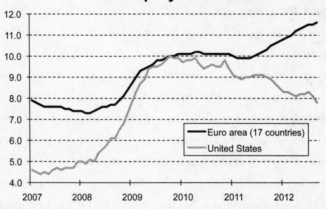

In the early phase, from late 2007 until early 2010, both Europe and America plunged into deep recession and experienced rapidly rising unemployment. The rise was sharper in the United States, where it's much easier to fire people than it is in most of Europe, but in any case the whole North Atlantic economy suffered the worst blow since the onset of the Great Depression.

Starting in 2010, however, the two sides of the Atlantic began to diverge. On one side, America started adding jobs. Although the initial fall in unemployment was partly a statistical illusion (as explained below), by 2011–12 a clear trend of economic improvement had emerged. The European economy, by contrast, went from bad to worse; by 2012 the continent was officially back in recession.

What accounts for this divergence? The explanation can be found in chapter 11, which describes how 2010 marked the sudden rise of the "Austerians," who insisted that governments impose spending cuts and tax hikes even in the face of high unemployment. In the United States, where Auste-

rian doctrine made only limited inroads, there was nonetheless some de facto austerity because of cutbacks by state
and local governments. In Europe, however, the Austerians
dominated the policy discussion. Savage austerity was made
a condition for aid to troubled debtor nations. To get a sense
of perspective, consider that if America were to undertake
spending cuts and tax hikes on the scale imposed on Greece,
they would amount to around $2.5 trillion *per year.* Mean-
while, countries that were having no trouble borrowing, like
Germany and the Netherlands, also imposed at least modest
austerity on themselves. So the overall result for Europe was
a sharp fiscal contraction.

According to Austerian doctrine, any negative effects from
this contraction should have been offset by an improvement in
consumer and business confidence—as I've put it, the "confidence fairy" was supposed to come to the rescue. In reality,
however, the confidence fairy failed to make an appearance.
The result is that while America has at least modestly recovered from the effects of the financial crisis, since 2010 Europe
has sunk even deeper into depression, with the pace of decline
increasing over the course of 2012.

Special mention should be given here to the United Kingdom,
which isn't on the euro and as a result has a great deal of policy
independence. Britain could have used that independence—
reflected, among other things, in very low borrowing costs—
to avoid getting caught up in the European debacle.
Unfortunately, the Cameron government, which came to
power in 2010, bought fully into Austerian doctrine, perhaps
more so than any other advanced-country regime. And while
there is some dispute about the relative importance of auster-

ity versus other factors in depressing the British economy, one thing is for sure: Britain's economy has performed remarkably badly, with GDP since the onset of the crisis trailing not just America but also the euro area and even Japan.

The good news, such as it is, is that at least some members of the policy elite have acknowledged that they got it wrong. In particular, the October 2012 edition of the International Monetary Fund's *World Economic Outlook* contained a striking mea culpa on the effects of austerity. The IMF acknowledged that after 2010 a number of European economies performed much worse than predicted; and it also acknowledged that these prediction errors were systematically related to austerity programs, with the countries that imposed the biggest spending cuts and/or tax increases falling the most below the forecast. The IMF's conclusion? Under depression-type conditions, "fiscal multipliers"—the effect of government expansion or contraction on the economy—are much bigger than the IMF and other agencies like the European Commission had thought. In fact, the IMF concluded that multipliers are more or less in line with what Keynesians had always claimed.

Unfortunately, at the time of this writing there is little sign that other key players in the European drama are willing to take this information on board. In Greece and in Portugal the "troika"—the IMF, the European Central Bank, and the European Commission—is still insisting on ever-harsher austerity as a condition for emergency loans, despite overwhelming evidence that the treatment is killing the patients. And while the central bank has declared itself willing in principle to buy the bonds of troubled nations like Spain and Italy, it has also made it clear that Spain, which is already engaged in

severe austerity, would have to do even more as a condition
for such purchases.

What would it take to save Europe? The recipe I offered in
chapter 10 is still the best hope: less savage austerity in debtor
countries, at least some fiscal expansion in creditor countries, and
expansionary policies from the European Central Bank that aim
at somewhat higher inflation for Europe as a whole. It's unclear,
however, whether or when such ideas will become politically
acceptable—and it's also not clear how much time Europe has.

For the continuing and worsening depression in Europe
isn't just a terrible human tragedy; it's also terrifying in its
political implications. In Greece radical political movements,
including the outright fascist Golden Dawn, are rising in influence. In Spain separatist movements, notably in Catalonia, are
on the rise. Nobody knows where the breaking point lies, but
the echoes of the 1930s are too strong to be ignored.

America's Partial Recovery

Since 2010, the United States has had two great advantages
compared with Europe. One is that our single currency is
backed by a single government, so that depressed regions
haven't faced European-style fiscal crises: Florida's housing
boom and bust weren't very different from Spain's, but Florida
can count on Washington to send its residents Social Security checks, pay its Medicare bills, and bail out its banks. As a
result, nothing like the financing crisis of southern Europe has
happened in America.

The other advantage is that the Austerians never gained
as much influence on this side of the Atlantic as they did in
Europe. It's true that they managed to shift economic debate
away from jobs and toward the alleged threat from the deficit—

a threat that, as explained in chapter 8, was always a figment of their imagination. (As Keynesians predicted, U.S. borrowing costs have remained at historic lows despite high debt and large deficits.) But the actual move toward austerity in America has been relatively modest, coming mainly from cutbacks at the state and local level.

The United States, in other words, has managed to avoid the severe policy mistakes afflicting Europe—and the U.S. economy has been making real if inadequate progress since late 2011. Unfortunately, that progress is endangered by a political deadlock that the 2012 election failed to resolve.

As the figure above shows, official U.S. unemployment is down substantially from its peak in late 2009. Some of the decline is a statistical illusion: workers are no longer considered unemployed if they're not actively looking for work, so sheer discouragement can reduce measured unemployment. From the fall of 2011 onward, however, there has been real, unmistakable improvement in the labor market, with employment among Americans of prime working age growing significantly faster than population.

These gains reflect the "natural healing process" described in chapter 12. Businesses are once again buying equipment and software, if only to keep up with advancing technology. Years of housing slump have worked off any excess construction during the bubble years, and housing is gradually recovering. And household debt has gradually declined relative to incomes, freeing consumers to begin a modest return to higher spending.

It's crucial, however, not to overstate the gains: the U.S. economy is still deeply depressed.

Consider, in particular, the problem of long-term unemployment, which is surely the worst scourge afflicting American workers. Before the financial crisis, we had very little long-term unemployment; although there were 6.8 million unemployed Americans in October 2007, only 750,000 had been out of work for more than a year. Four years later, that number had risen almost sixfold, to 4.1 million; and despite the signs of recovery, in October 2012 there were still 3.6 million Americans in the year-plus-unemployed category.

The point is that while the U.S. economy is making progress, the progress is far slower than it should be, and there is still enormous, unnecessary suffering among American workers and their families. And there's a real risk that political deadlock may undermine even this inadequate recovery, thanks to the "fiscal cliff."

Actually, that phrase, coined by Ben Bernanke, is turning out to be problematic, because it makes some people believe, wrongly, that the looming problem is connected to the budget deficit. I prefer a term proposed by Brian Beutler of the website Talking Points Memo: the "austerity bomb," a bomb whose fuse was lit by two acts of right-wing partisanship.

First, back in 2001 the then president George W. Bush rammed a large tax cut through Congress, exploiting the parliamentary maneuver known as reconciliation to bypass a Senate filibuster. By Senate rules, tax legislation passed by means of that maneuver had to expire at the end of 2010; Bush didn't mind, partly because he expected Republicans to still be in control when the deadline rolled around, partly because the cutoff date concealed the true budget cost of his giveaway.

As it turned out, however, when December 31, 2010 arrived, a Democrat was in the White House. Still, rather than see taxes go up in the face of a depressed economy, President Obama cut a deal extending the Bush tax cuts a further two years. Now that the election is behind him, however, he wants to let some of the cuts—those benefiting the wealthiest Americans—expire. Yet Republicans still control the House and are currently threatening to block any tax legislation unless it keeps rates on the rich low. If the impasse isn't resolved, taxes on the middle class as well as the rich will go up, imposing a significant blow at a time when the economy is still depressed.

On top of this, in 2011 Republicans threatened to block a needed rise in the U.S. debt ceiling, thereby preventing the government from borrowing the money it needed to pay its bills. To avoid this outcome, which might have been disastrous, they demanded policy concessions—and the president chose not to call their bluff, instead negotiating a deal that would slash spending at the end of 2012 unless further agreement was reached. No such agreement had been reached at the time of this writing.

Oh, and on top of all this, several important pieces of economic stimulus—mainly a temporary cut in the payroll tax and extended unemployment benefits—are also set to expire at the end of 2012.

What all this means is that if political gridlock continues, the U.S. government will more or less automatically engage in a sudden bout of European-style austerity, raising taxes and slashing spending in a weak economy. That is definitely not what the doctor ordered.

Yet it may happen anyway. From President Obama's point of view, he's facing attempted blackmail: Republicans are threatening to blow up the economy unless he gives them what they want. He effectively gave in to such blackmail at the end of 2010 and again in 2011 over the debt ceiling; if he's ever going to take a stand, it would be hard to pick a better time than immediately following his triumphant reelection. And taking off my macroeconomics hat, I would personally encourage him to call the GOP's bluff. The short-term macroeconomic impact might not be pretty, but there are larger issues at stake.

Meanwhile, Republicans may have suffered a major defeat, but they still hold the House. And while business interests badly want a deal to avoid the austerity bomb, the hard right—which is angry and bitter over failing to topple the president, and looking for revenge—retains a strong grip on the party.

All this suggests that it's quite possible that no deal will be reached before the end of 2012. That needn't be a disaster: another problem with the "fiscal cliff" language is that it suggests, wrongly, that even a brief failure to reach a deal would be catastrophic. The truth is that we could probably go several months into 2013 with only minor economic damage. My guess—and it's only a guess, which may well have been proved wrong by the time you read this—is that we will in fact go some way into 2013 before reaching a deal, but that pressure from the business community will basically force the GOP to give in to the president before serious harm is done.

Even if that happens, however, the underlying economic story will remain deeply unsatisfactory: America will continue its gradual recovery, but that will still mean years of gratuitous suffering and economic waste. So what can and should be done?

Ways Forward

America is still an economy in depression, and the rules of depression economics still apply: what we need, above all, is more spending, to put unemployed workers and idle productive capacity to work. And the best, most surefire way to do that is to have the government spend more—which, as I say in this book, could be easily accomplished simply by providing enough aid to state and local governments to let them rehire those hundreds of thousands of schoolteachers, repair those potholed roads, and so on.

Unfortunately, the political scene isn't as favorable as one might have hoped. Republicans still control the House, and while they may have been shaken by their failure to take the White House and the Senate, they're not going to be easily persuaded to do the right thing. What else can be done?

One answer is that the Fed needs to do more. Back in 2000, when Japan was suffering from an extended slump, a professor named Ben Bernanke called on the Bank of Japan to show "Rooseveltian resolve," to do whatever it took to get the economy moving again. As I explain in the book, it has been a major disappointment that this kind of resolve seemed sadly lacking once Professor Bernanke, now Federal Reserve Chairman Bernanke, had to confront a similar situation in America. But there are signs that the Fed is finally getting on the case—perhaps freed by the election from fears that it would be accused of revving up the economy to help the Obama campaign.

So far, at least, the Fed has taken only partial steps toward a more aggressive policy. The key, according to most analyses, is for the Fed to convince investors that it will allow somewhat higher inflation in the medium term. And while it seems to be moving in that direction, at this point those moves take the form of vague indications rather than firm commitments. The good news is that the inflation worriers seem to be in retreat, and the Fed looks increasingly willing to take risks for full employment.

That said, the Fed probably can't engineer a full recovery on its own. It needs help. And some of that help can come from debt relief. In particular, the Federal Housing Finance Agency, which oversees Fannie Mae and Freddie Mac, still retains the ability to provide widespread debt relief with a stroke of the pen. All it has to do is waive the down payment requirements for refinancing of Fannie/Freddie-owned mortgages, and millions of homeowners can quickly reduce their interest burden by refinancing at much lower rates.

Finally, while the road to fiscal stimulus may be politically difficult, that's no reason to give up. Indeed, a number of Democrats in Congress are demanding that some kind of short-term economic boost be included as part of any deal on the austerity bomb; this is a really good idea. And as 2013 proceeds, President Obama should make the case, repeatedly, that Republican obstruction is standing in the way of job creation, and demand that the GOP get out of the way.

For this depression is far from over, even though there is no good reason for it to persist. True, there's still a political and ideological logjam blocking the policies that could bring a rapid recovery. But that logjam seems to be gradually breaking up—and it's the responsibility of everyone who has a public voice to accelerate that process, and bring relief to the long-suffering unemployed. We have the tools; all we need is the intellectual clarity and the will. It's still in our power to end this depression—now.

INTRODUCTION

WHAT DO WE DO NOW?

THIS IS A BOOK about the economic slump now afflicting the United States and many other countries—a slump that has now entered its fifth year and that shows no signs of ending anytime soon. Needless to say, many books about the financial crisis of 2008, which marked the beginning of the slump, have already been published, and many more are no doubt in the pipeline. But this book is, I believe, different from most of those other books, because it tries to answer a different question. For the most part, the mushrooming literature on our economic disaster asks, "How did this happen?" My question, instead, is "What do we do now?"

Obviously these are somewhat related questions, but they are by no means identical. Knowing what causes heart attacks is not at all the same thing as knowing how to treat them; the same is true of economic crises. And right now the question of treatment should be what concerns us most. Every time I read some academic or opinion article discussing what we should be doing to prevent future financial crises—and I read many such articles—I get a bit impatient. Yes, it's a worthy question, but since we have yet to recover from the last crisis, shouldn't achieving recovery be our first priority?

For we are still very much living in the shadow of the economic catastrophe that struck both Europe and the United States four years ago. Gross domestic product, which normally grows a couple of percent a year, is barely above its precrisis peak even in countries that have seen a relatively strong recovery, and it is down by double digits in several European nations. Meanwhile, unemployment on both sides of the Atlantic remains at levels that would have seemed inconceivable before the crisis.

The best way to think about this continued slump, I'd argue, is to accept the fact that we're in a depression. No, it's not the Great Depression, at least not for most of us (but talk to the Greeks, the Irish, or even the Spaniards, who have 23 percent unemployment—and almost 50 percent unemployment among the young). But it's nonetheless essentially the same kind of situation that John Maynard Keynes described in the 1930s: "a chronic condition of subnormal activity for a considerable period without any marked tendency either towards recovery or towards complete collapse."

And that's not an acceptable condition. There are some economists and policy officials who seem satisfied with avoiding "complete collapse"; but the reality is that this "chronic condition of subnormal activity," reflected above all in a lack of jobs, is inflicting enormous, cumulative human damage.

So it's extremely important that we take action to promote a real, full recovery. And here's the thing: we know how to do that, or at least we *should* know how to do that. We are suffering woes that, for all the differences in detail that come with seventy-five years of economic, technological, and social change, are recognizably similar to those of the 1930s. And we know what policy makers should have been doing then, both from the contemporary analysis of Keynes and others and from much subsequent research and analysis. That same analysis tells us what we should be doing in our current predicament.

Unfortunately, we're not using the knowledge we have, because too many people who matter—politicians, public officials, and the broader class of writers and talkers who define conventional wisdom—have, for a variety of reasons, chosen to forget the lessons of history and the conclusions of several generations' worth of economic analysis, replacing that hard-won knowledge with ideologically and politically convenient prejudices. Above all, conventional wisdom among what some of us have taken to referring to, sarcastically, as Very Serious People has completely thrown away Keynes's central dictum: "The boom, not the slump, is the time for austerity." Now is the time for the government to spend more, not less, until the private sector is ready to carry the economy forward again—yet job-destroying austerity policies have instead become the rule.

This book, then, attempts to break the hold of that destructive conventional wisdom and to make the case for the expansionary, job-creating policies we should have been following all along. To make that case I need to present evidence; yes, this book has charts in it. But I hope that this doesn't make it seem technical, or keep it from being accessible to intelligent lay readers, even if economics is not their usual thing. For

what I'm trying to do here is, in effect, to go over the heads of
the Serious People who have, for whatever reason, taken all of
us down the wrong path, at immense cost to our economies
and our societies, and to appeal to informed public opinion in
an effort to get us doing the right thing instead.

Maybe, just maybe, our economies will be on a rapid path
to true recovery by the time this book reaches the shelves, and
this appeal won't be necessary. I surely hope so—but I very
much doubt it. Instead, all indications are that the economy
will remain weak for a very long time unless our policy makers change course. And my aim here is to bring pressure, by
means of an informed public, to get that course change, and
bring an end to this depression.

End
This Depression
Now!

CHAPTER ONE

HOW BAD THINGS ARE

I think as those green shoots begin to appear in different markets and as some confidence begins to come back that will begin the positive dynamic that brings our economy back.
  Do you see green shoots?
  I do. I do see green shoots.

—Ben Bernanke, chairman of the Federal Reserve,
interviewed by *60 Minutes*, March 15, 2009

IN MARCH 2009 Ben Bernanke, normally neither the most cheerful nor the most poetic of men, waxed optimistic about the economic prospect. After the fall of Lehman Brothers six months earlier, America had entered a terrifying economic nosedive. But appearing on the TV show *60 Minutes*, the Fed chairman declared that spring was at hand.

His remarks immediately became famous, not least because they bore an eerie resemblance to the words of Chance, aka Chauncey Gardiner, the simpleminded gardener mistaken for a wise man in the movie *Being There*. In one scene Chance, asked to comment on economic policy, assures the president, "As long as the roots are not severed, all is well and all will be well in the garden. . . . There will be growth in the spring." Despite the jokes, however, Bernanke's optimism was widely shared. And at the end of 2009 *Time* declared Bernanke its Person of the Year.

Unfortunately, all was not well in the garden, and the promised growth never came.

To be fair, Bernanke was right that the crisis was easing. The panic that had gripped financial markets was ebbing, and the economy's plunge was slowing. According to the official scorekeepers at the National Bureau of Economic Research, the so-called Great Recession that started in December 2007 ended in June 2009, and recovery began. But if it was a recovery, it was one that did little to help most Americans. Jobs remained scarce; more and more families depleted their savings, lost their homes, and, worst of all, lost hope. True, the unemployment rate is down from the peak it reached in October 2009. But progress has come at a snail's pace; we're still waiting, after all these years, for that "positive dynamic" Bernanke talked about to make an appearance.

And that was in America, which at least had a technical recovery. Other countries didn't even manage that. In Ireland, in Greece, in Spain, in Italy, debt problems and the "austerity" programs that were supposed to restore confidence not only aborted any kind of recovery but produced renewed slumps and soaring unemployment.

And the pain went on and on. I'm writing these words almost three years after Bernanke thought he saw those green shoots, three and a half years after Lehman fell, more than four years after the start of the Great Recession. The citizens of the world's most advanced nations, nations rich in resources, talent, and knowledge—all the ingredients for prosperity and a decent standard of living for all—remain in a state of intense pain.

In the rest of this chapter I'll try to document some of

the main dimensions of that pain. I'll focus mainly on the United States, which is both my home and the country I know best, reserving an extended discussion of the pain abroad for later in the book. And I'll start with the thing that matters most—and the thing on which we've performed the worst: unemployment.

The Jobs Drought

Economists, the old line goes, know the price of everything and the value of nothing. And you know what? There's a lot of truth to that accusation: since economists mainly study the circulation of money and the production and consumption of stuff, they have an inherent bias toward assuming that money and stuff are what matter. Still, there is a field of economic research that focuses on how self-reported measures of well-being, such as happiness or "life satisfaction," are related to other aspects of life. Yes, it's known as "happiness research"—Ben Bernanke even gave a speech about it in 2010, titled "The Economics of Happiness." And this research tells us something very important about the mess we're in.

Sure enough, happiness research tells us that money isn't all that important once you get to the point of being able to afford the necessities of life. The payoff to being richer isn't literally zero—citizens of rich countries are, on average, somewhat more satisfied with their lives than citizens of less well-off nations. Also, being richer or poorer than the people you compare yourself with is a fairly big deal, which is why extreme inequality can have such a corrosive effect on society. But when all is said and done, money is less important than crude materialists—and many economists—would like to believe.

That's not to say, however, that economic affairs are unimportant in the true scale of things. For there's one economics-driven thing that matters enormously to human well-being: having a job. People who want to work but can't find work suffer greatly, not just from the loss of income but from a diminished sense of self-worth. And that's a major reason why mass unemployment—which has now been going on in America for four years—is such a tragedy.

How severe is the problem of unemployment? That question calls for a bit of discussion.

Clearly, what we're interested in is *involuntary* unemployment. People who aren't working because they have chosen not to work, or at least not to work in the market economy— retirees who are glad to be retired, or those who have decided to be full-time housewives or househusbands—don't count. Neither do the disabled, whose inability to work is unfortunate, but not driven by economic issues.

Now, there have always been people claiming that there's no such thing as involuntary unemployment, that anyone can find a job if he or she is really willing to work and isn't too finicky about wages or working conditions. There's Sharron Angle, the Republican candidate for the Senate, who declared in 2010 that the unemployed were "spoiled," choosing to live off unemployment benefits instead of taking jobs. There are the people at the Chicago Board of Trade who, in October 2011, mocked anti-inequality demonstrators by showering them with copies of McDonald's job application forms. And there are economists like the University of Chicago's Casey Mulligan, who has written multiple articles for the *New York Times* website insisting that the sharp drop in employment after the 2008 financial crisis reflected not a lack of employment opportunities but diminished willingness to work.

The classic answer to such people comes from a passage near the beginning of the novel *The Treasure of the Sierra Madre* (best known for the 1948 film adaptation starring Humphrey Bogart and Walter Huston): "Anyone who is willing to work and is serious about it will certainly find a job. Only you must not go to the man who tells you this, for he has no job to offer and doesn't know anyone who knows of a vacancy. This is exactly the reason why he gives you such generous advice, out of brotherly love, and to demonstrate how little he knows the world."

Quite. Also, about those McDonald's applications: in April 2011, as it happens, McDonald's did announce 50,000 new job openings. Roughly a million people applied.

If you have any familiarity with the world, in short, you know that involuntary unemployment is very real. And it's currently a very big deal.

How bad is the problem of involuntary unemployment, and how much worse has it become?

The U.S. unemployment measure you usually hear quoted in the news is based on a survey in which adults are asked whether they are either working or actively seeking work. Those who are seeking work but don't have jobs are considered unemployed. In December 2011 that amounted to more than 13 million Americans, up from 6.8 million in 2007.

If you think about it, however, this standard definition of unemployment misses a lot of distress. What about people who want to work, but aren't actively searching either because there are no jobs to be had, or because they've grown discouraged by fruitless searching? What about those who want full-time work, but have only been able to find part-time jobs? Well, the U.S. Bureau of Labor Statistics tries to capture these unfortunates in a broader measure of unemployment, known as U6;

it says that by this broader measure there are about 24 million unemployed Americans—about 15 percent of the workforce—roughly double the number before the crisis.

Yet even this measure fails to capture the extent of the pain. In modern America most families contain two working spouses; such families suffer, both financially and psychologically, if either spouse is unemployed. There are workers who used to make ends meet with a second job, now down to an inadequate one, or who counted on overtime pay that no longer arrives. There are independent businesspeople who have seen their income shrivel. There are skilled workers, accustomed to holding down good jobs, who have been forced to accept work that uses none of their skills. And on and on.

There is no official estimate of the number of Americans caught up in this sort of penumbra of formal unemployment. But in a June 2011 poll of likely voters—a group probably in better shape than the population as a whole—the polling group Democracy Corps found that a third of Americans had either themselves suffered from job loss or had a family member lose a job, and that another third knew someone who had lost a job. Moreover, almost 40 percent of families had suffered from reduced hours, wages, or benefits.

The pain, then, is very widespread. But that's not the whole story: for millions, the damage from the bad economy runs very deep.

Ruined Lives

There is always some unemployment in a complex, dynamic economy like that of modern America. Every day some businesses fail, taking jobs with them, while others grow and need more staff; workers quit or are fired for idiosyncratic reasons, and their former employers take on replacements. In 2007, when the job market was pretty good, more than 20 million workers quit or were fired, while an even larger number were hired.

All this churning means that some unemployment remains even when times are good, because it often takes time before would-be workers find or accept new jobs. As we saw, there were almost seven million unemployed workers in the fall of 2007 despite a fairly prosperous economy. There were millions of unemployed Americans even at the height of the 1990s boom, when the joke was that anyone who could pass the "mirror test"—that is, anyone whose breath would fog a mirror, indicating that they were actually alive—could find work.

In times of prosperity, however, unemployment is mostly a brief experience. In good times there is a rough match between the number of people seeking work and the number of job openings, and as a result most of the unemployed find work fairly quickly. Of those seven million unemployed Americans before the crisis, fewer than one in five had been out of work as much as six months, fewer than one in ten had been out of work for a year or more.

That situation has changed completely since the crisis. There are now four job seekers for every job opening, which means that workers who lose one job find it very hard to get another. Six million Americans, almost five times as many as in 2007, have been out of work for six months or more; four million have been out of work for more than a year, up from just 700,000 before the crisis.

This is something almost completely new in American experience—I say *almost* completely, because long-term unemployment was obviously rife during the Great Depression. But there's been nothing like this since. Not since the 1930s have so many Americans found themselves seemingly trapped in a permanent state of joblessness.

Long-term unemployment is deeply demoralizing for workers anywhere. In America, where the social safety net is weaker than in any other advanced country, it can easily become a nightmare. Losing your job often means losing your health insurance. Unemployment benefits, which typically make up only about a third of lost income anyway, run out—over the course of 2010–11 there was a slight fall in the official unemployment rate, but the number of Americans who were unemployed yet receiving no benefits doubled. And as unemployment drags on, household finances fall apart—family savings are depleted, bills can't be paid, homes are lost.

Nor is that all. The causes of long-term unemployment clearly lie with macroeconomic events and policy failures that are beyond any individual's control, yet that does not save the victims from bearing a stigma. Does being unemployed for a long time really erode work skills, and make you a poor hire? Does the fact that you were one of the long-term unemployed indicate that you were a loser in the first place? Maybe not, but many employers *think* it does, and for the worker that may be all that matters. Lose a job in this economy, and it's very hard to find another; stay unemployed long enough, and you will be considered unemployable.

To all this add the damage to Americans' inner lives. You know what I mean if you know anyone trapped in long-term unemployment; even if he or she isn't in financial distress, the blow to dignity and self-respect can be devastating. And matters are, of course, worse if there is financial distress too. When Ben Bernanke spoke about "happiness research," he emphasized the finding that happiness depends strongly on a sense of being in control of your own life. Think about what happens to that sense of being in control when you want to work, yet many months have gone by and you can't find a job, when the life you built is falling apart because funds are running out. It's no wonder that the evidence suggests that long-term unemployment breeds anxiety and psychological depression.

Meanwhile, there's the plight of those who don't have a job yet, because they're entering the working world for the first time. Truly, this is a terrible time to be young.

Unemployment among young workers, like unemployment for just about every demographic group, roughly doubled in the immediate aftermath of the crisis, then drifted down a bit. But because young workers have a much higher unemployment rate than their elders even in good times, this meant a much larger rise in unemployment relative to the workforce.

And the young workers one might have expected to be best placed to weather the crisis—recent college graduates, who presumably are much more likely than others to have the knowledge and skills a modern economy demands—were by no means insulated. Roughly one in four recent graduates is either unemployed or working only part-time. There has also been a notable drop in wages for those who do have full-time jobs, probably because many of them have had to take low-paying jobs that don't make use of their education.

One more thing: there has been a sharp increase in the number of Americans aged between twenty-four and thirty-four living with their parents. This doesn't represent a sudden rush of filial devotion; it represents a radical reduction in opportunities to leave the nest.

This situation is deeply frustrating for young people. They're supposed to be getting on with their lives, but instead they find themselves in a holding pattern. Many understandably worry about their future. How long a shadow will their current problems cast? When can they expect to fully recover from the bad luck of graduating into a deeply troubled economy?

Basically, never. Lisa Kahn, an economist at Yale's School of Management, has compared the careers of college graduates who received their degrees in years of high unemployment with those who graduated in boom times; the graduates with unlucky timing did significantly worse, not just in the few years after graduation but for their whole working lives. And those past eras of high unemployment were relatively short compared with what we're experiencing now, suggesting that the long-term damage to the lives of young Americans will be much greater this time around.

Dollars and Cents

Money? Did someone mention money? So far, I haven't, at least not directly. And that's deliberate. Although the disaster we're living through is in large part a story of markets and money, a tale of getting and spending gone wrong, what makes it a disaster is the human dimension, not the money lost.

That having been said, we're talking about a lot of money lost.

The measure most commonly used to track overall economic performance is real gross domestic product, or real GDP for short. It's the total value of goods and services produced in an economy, adjusted for inflation; roughly speaking, it's the amount of stuff (including services, of course) that the economy makes in a given period of time. Since income comes from selling stuff, it's also the total amount of income earned, determining the size of the pie that gets sliced between wages, profits, and taxes.

In an average year before the crisis, America's real GDP grew between 2 and 2.5 percent per year. That's because the economy's productive capacity was growing over time: each year there were more willing workers, more machines and structures for those workers to use, and more sophisticated technology to be employed. There were occasional setbacks— recessions—in which the economy briefly shrank instead of growing. I'll talk in the next chapter about why and how that can happen. But these setbacks were normally brief and small, and were followed by bursts of growth as the economy made up the lost ground.

Until the recent crisis, the worst setback experienced by the U.S. economy since the Great Depression was the "double dip" of 1979 to 1982—two recessions in close succession that are best viewed as basically a single slump with a stutter in the middle. At the bottom of that slump, in late 1982, real GDP was 2 percent below its previous peak. But the economy proceeded to bounce back strongly, growing at a 7 percent rate for the next two years—"morning in America"—and then returned to its normal growth track.

The Great Recession—the plunge between late 2007 and the middle of 2009, when the economy stabilized—was steeper and sharper, with real GDP falling 5 percent over the course of eighteen months. More important, however, there has been no strong bounce-back. Growth since the official end of the recession has actually been lower than normal. The result is an economy producing far less than it should.

The Congressional Budget Office (CBO) produces a widely used estimate of "potential" real GDP, defined as a measure of "sustainable output, in which the intensity of resource use is neither adding to nor subtracting from inflationary pressure." Think of it as what would happen if the economic engine were firing on all cylinders but not overheating—an estimate of what we could and should be achieving. It's pretty close to what you get if you take where the U.S. economy was in 2007, and project what it would be producing now if growth had continued at its long-run average pace.

Some economists argue that estimates like this are misleading, that we've taken a major hit to our productive capacity; I'll explain in chapter 2 why I disagree. For now, however, let's take the CBO estimate at face value. What it says is that as I write these words the U.S. economy is operating about 7 percent below its potential. Or to put it a bit differently, we're currently producing around a trillion dollars less of value each year than we could and should be producing.

That's an amount *per year*. If you add up the lost value since the slump began, it comes to some $3 trillion. Given the economy's continuing weakness, that number is set to get a lot bigger. At this point we'll be very lucky if we get away with a cumulative output loss of "only" $5 trillion.

These aren't paper losses like the wealth lost when the dot-com or housing bubble collapsed, wealth that was never real in the first place. We're talking here about valuable products that could and should have been manufactured but weren't, wages and profits that could and should have been earned but never materialized. And that's $5 trillion, or $7 trillion, or maybe even more that we'll never get back. The economy will eventually recover, one hopes—but that will, at best, mean getting back to its old trend line, not making up for all the years it spent below that trend line

I say "at best" advisedly, because there are good reasons to believe that the prolonged weakness of the economy will take a toll on its long-run potential.

Losing the Future

Amid all the excuses you hear for not taking action to end this depression, one refrain is repeated constantly by apologists for inaction: we need, they say, to focus on the long run, not the short run.

This is wrong on multiple levels, as we'll see later in this book. Among other things, it involves an intellectual abdication, a refusal to accept responsibility for understanding the current depression; it's tempting and easy to wave all this unpleasantness away and talk airily about the long run, but that's taking the lazy, cowardly way out. John Maynard Keynes was making exactly this point when he wrote one of his most famous passages: "This *long run* is a misleading guide to current affairs. *In the long run* we are all dead. Economists set themselves too easy, too useless a task if in tempestuous seasons they can only tell us that when the storm is long past the sea is flat again."

Focusing only on the long run means ignoring the vast suffering the current depression is inflicting, the lives it is ruining irreparably as you read this. But that's not all. Our short-run problems—if you can call a slump now in its fifth year "short-run"—are hurting our long-run prospects too, through multiple channels.

I've already mentioned a couple of those channels. One is the corrosive effect of long-term unemployment: if workers who have been jobless for extended periods come to be seen as unemployable, that's a long-term reduction in the economy's effective workforce, and hence in its productive capacity. The plight of college graduates forced to take jobs that don't use their skills is somewhat similar: as time goes by, they may find themselves demoted, at least in the eyes of potential employ-ers, to the status of low-skilled workers, which will mean that their education goes to waste.

A second way in which the slump undermines our future is through low business investment. Businesses aren't spend-ing much on expanding their capacity; in fact, manufactur-ing capacity has fallen about 5 percent since the start of the Great Recession, as companies have scrapped older capacity and not installed new capacity to replace it. A lot of mythology surrounds low business investment—It's uncertainty! It's fear of that socialist in the White House!—but there's no actual mystery: investment is low because businesses aren't selling enough to use the capacity they already have.

The problem is that if and when the economy finally does recover, it will bump up against capacity limits and production bottlenecks much sooner than it would have if the persistent slump hadn't given businesses every reason to stop investing in the future.

Last but not least, the way the economic crisis has been (mis)handled means that public programs that serve the future are being savaged.

Educating the young is crucial for the twenty-first cen-tury—so say all the politicians and pundits. Yet the ongoing slump, by creating a fiscal crisis for state and local govern-ments, has led to the laying off of some 300,000 schoolteach-ers. The same fiscal crisis has led state and local governments to postpone or cancel investments in transportation and water infrastructure, like the desperately needed second rail tunnel under the Hudson River, the high-speed rail projects canceled in Wisconsin, Ohio, and Florida, the light-rail projects canceled in a number of cities, and so on. Adjusted for inflation, public investment has fallen sharply since the slump began. Again, this means that if and when the economy finally does recover, we'll run into bottlenecks and shortages far too soon.

How much should these sacrifices of the future worry us? The International Monetary Fund has studied the aftermath of past financial crises in a number of countries, and its findings are deeply disturbing: not only do such crises inflict severe short-run damage; they seem to take a huge long-term toll as well, with growth and employment shifted more or less permanently onto a lower track. And here's the thing: the evidence suggests that effective action to limit the depth and duration of the slump after a financial crisis reduces this long-run damage too—which means, conversely, that failing to take such action, which is what we're doing now, also means accepting a diminished, embittered future.

Pain Abroad

Up to this point I've been talking about America, for two obvious reasons: it's my country, so its pain hurts me most, and it's also the country I know best. But America's pain is by no means unique.

Europe, in particular, presents an equally dismaying picture. In aggregate, Europe has suffered an employment slump that's not quite as bad as America's, but terrible all the same; in terms of gross domestic product, Europe has actually done worse. Moreover, the European experience is highly uneven across nations. Although Germany is relatively unscathed (so far—but watch what happens next), the European periphery is facing utter disaster. In particular, if this is a terrible time to be young in America, with its 17 percent unemployment rate among those under twenty-five, it's a nightmare in Italy, where the youth unemployment rate is 28 percent, in Ireland, where it's 30 percent, and in Spain, where it's 43 percent.

The good news about Europe, such as it is, is that because European nations have much stronger social safety nets than the United States, the immediate consequences of unemployment are much less severe. Universal health care means that losing your job in Europe doesn't mean losing health insurance too; relatively generous unemployment benefits mean that hunger and homelessness are not as prevalent.

But Europe's awkward combination of unity and disunity— the adoption by most nations of a common currency without having created the kind of political and economic union that such a common currency demands—has become a gigantic source of weakness and renewed crisis.

In Europe, as in America, the slump has hit regions unevenly; the places that had the biggest bubbles before the crisis are having the biggest slumps now—think of Spain as being Europe's Florida, Ireland as being Europe's Nevada. But the Florida legislature doesn't have to worry about coming up with the funds to pay for Medicare and Social Security, which are paid for by the federal government; Spain is on its own, as are Greece, Portugal, and Ireland. So in Europe the depressed economy has caused fiscal crises, in which private investors are no longer willing to lend to a number of countries. And the response to these fiscal crises—frantic, savage attempts to slash spending—has pushed unemployment all around Europe's periphery to Great Depression levels, and seems at the time of writing to be pushing Europe back into outright recession.

The Politics of Despair

The ultimate costs of the Great Depression went far beyond economic losses, or even the suffering associated with mass unemployment. The Depression had catastrophic political effects as well. In particular, while modern conventional wisdom links the rise of Hitler to the German hyperinflation of 1923, what actually brought him to power was the German depression of the early 1930s, a depression that was even more severe than that in the rest of Europe, thanks to the deflationary policies of Chancellor Heinrich Brüning.

Can anything like that happen today? There's a well-established and justified stigma attached to invoking Nazi parallels (look up "Godwin's law"), and it's hard to see anything quite that bad happening in the twenty-first century. Yet it would be foolish to minimize the dangers a prolonged slump poses to democratic values and institutions. There has in fact been a clear rise in extremist politics across the Western world: radical anti-immigrant movements, radical nationalist movements, and, yes, authoritarian sentiments are all on the march. Indeed, one Western nation, Hungary, already seems well on its way toward reverting to an authoritarian regime reminiscent of those that spread across much of Europe in the 1930s.

Nor is America immune. Can anyone deny that the Republican Party has become far more extreme over the past few years? And it has a reasonable chance of taking both Congress and the White House later this year, despite its radicalism, because extremism flourishes in an environment in which respectable voices offer no solutions as the population suffers.

Don't Give Up

I've just painted a portrait of immense human disaster. But disasters do happen; history is replete with floods and famines, earthquakes and tsunamis. What makes this disaster so terrible—what should make you *angry*—is that none of this need be happening. There has been no plague of locusts; we have not lost our technological know-how; America and Europe should be richer, not poorer, than they were five years ago.

Nor is the nature of the disaster mysterious. In the Great Depression leaders had an excuse: nobody really understood what was happening or how to fix it. Today's leaders don't have that excuse. *We have both the knowledge and the tools to end this suffering.*

Yet we aren't doing it. In the chapters that follow I'll try to explain why—how a combination of self-interest and distorted ideology has prevented us from solving a solvable problem. And I have to admit that watching us fail so completely to do what should be done occasionally gives me a sense of despair.

But that's the wrong reaction.

As the slump has gone on and on, I have found myself listening often to a beautiful song originally performed in the 1980s by Peter Gabriel and Kate Bush. The song is set in an unidentified time and place of mass unemployment; the despairing male voice sings of his hopelessness: "For every job, so many men." But the female voice encourages him: "Don't give up."

These are terrible times, and all the more terrible because it's all so unnecessary. But don't give up: we can end this depression, if we can only find the clarity and the will.

CHAPTER TWO

DEPRESSION ECONOMICS

The world has been slow to realise that we are living this year in the shadow of one of the greatest economic catastrophes of modern history. But now that the man in the street has become aware of what is happening, he, not knowing the why and wherefore, is as full to-day of what may prove excessive fears as, previously, when the trouble was first coming on, he was lacking in what would have been a reasonable anxiety. He begins to doubt the future. Is he now awakening from a pleasant dream to face the darkness of facts? Or dropping off into a nightmare which will pass away?

He need not be doubtful. The other was not a dream. This is a nightmare, which will pass away with the morning. For the resources of Nature and men's devices are just as fertile and productive as they were. The rate of our progress towards solving the material problems of life is not less rapid. We are as capable as before of affording for every one a high standard of life—high, I mean, compared with, say, twenty years ago—and will soon learn to afford a standard higher still. We were not previously deceived. But to-day we have involved ourselves in a colossal muddle, having blundered in the control of a delicate machine, the working of which we do not understand. The result is that our possibilities of wealth may run to waste for a time—perhaps for a long time.

—John Maynard Keynes, "The Great Slump of 1930"

THE WORDS ABOVE were written more than eighty years ago, as the world was descending into what would later be dubbed the Great Depression. Yet, aside from a few archaisms of style, they could have been written today. Now, as then, we live in the shadow of economic catastrophe. Now, as then, we have suddenly become poorer—yet neither our resources nor our knowledge have been impaired, so where does this sudden poverty come from? Now, as then, it seems as if our possibilities of wealth may run to waste for a long time.

How can this be happening? Actually, it's not a mystery. We understand—or we *would* understand, if so many weren't refusing to listen—how these things happen. Keynes provided much of the analytical framework needed to make sense of depressions; modern economics can also draw on the insights of his contemporaries John Hicks and Irving Fisher, insights that have been expanded and made more sophisticated by a number of modern economists.

The central message of all this work is that *this doesn't have to be happening.* In that same essay Keynes declared that the economy was suffering from "magneto trouble," an old-fashioned term for problems with a car's electrical system. A more modern and arguably more accurate analogy might be that we've suffered a software crash. Either way, the point is that the problem isn't with the economic engine, which is as powerful as ever. Instead, we're talking about what is basically a technical problem, a problem of organization and coordination—a "colossal muddle," as Keynes put it. Solve this technical problem, and the economy will roar back to life.

Now, many people find this message fundamentally implausible, even offensive. It seems only natural to suppose that large problems must have large causes, that mass unemployment must be the result of something deeper than a mere muddle. That's why Keynes used his magneto analogy. We all know that sometimes a $100 battery replacement is all it takes to get a stalled $30,000 car back on the road, and he hoped to convince readers that a similar disproportion between cause and effect can apply to depressions. But this point was and is hard for many people, including those who believe themselves well-informed, to accept.

Partly that's because it just feels wrong to attribute such devastation to a relatively minor malfunction. Partly, too, there's a strong desire to see economics as a morality play, in which bad times are the ineluctable punishment for previous excesses. In 2010 my wife and I had the opportunity to hear a speech on economic policy by Wolfgang Schäuble, the German finance minister; midway through, she leaned over and whispered, "As we leave the room, we'll be given whips to scourge ourselves." Schäuble is, admittedly, even more of a fire-and-brimstone preacher than most financial officials, but many share his tendencies. And the people who say such things—who sagely declare that our problems have deep roots and no easy solution, that we all have to adjust to a more austere outlook—sound wise and realistic, even though they're utterly wrong.

What I hope to do in this chapter is convince you that we do, in fact, have magneto trouble. The sources of our suffering are relatively trivial in the scheme of things, and could be fixed quickly and fairly easily if enough people in positions of power understood the realities. Moreover, for the great majority of people the process of fixing the economy would *not* be painful and involve sacrifices; on the contrary, ending this depression would be a feel-good experience for almost everyone except those who are politically, emotionally, and professionally invested in wrongheaded economic doctrines.

Now, let me be clear: in saying that the causes of our economic disaster are relatively trivial, I am not saying that they emerged at random or came out of thin air. Nor am I saying that it's easy as a *political* matter to get ourselves out of this mess. It took decades of bad policies and bad ideas to get us into this depression—bad policies and bad ideas that, as we'll see in chapter 4, flourished because for a long time they worked very well, not for the nation as a whole but for a handful of very wealthy, very influential people. And those bad policies and bad ideas have a powerful grip on our political culture, making it very hard to change course even in the face of economic catastrophe. As a purely economic matter, however, this crisis isn't hard to solve; we could have a quick, powerful recovery if only we could find the intellectual clarity and political will to act.

Think of it this way: suppose that your husband has, for whatever reason, refused to maintain the family car's electrical system over the years. Now the car won't start, but he refuses even to consider replacing the battery, in part because that would mean admitting that he was wrong before, and he insists instead that the family must learn to walk and take buses. Clearly, you have a problem, and it may even be an insoluble problem as far as you are concerned. But it's a problem with your husband, not with the family car, which could and should be easily fixed.

OK, enough metaphors. Let's talk about what has gone wrong with the world economy.

It's All about Demand

Why is unemployment so high, and economic output so low? Because we—where by "we" I mean consumers, businesses, and governments combined—aren't spending enough. Spending on home construction and consumer goods plunged when the twin housing bubbles in America and Europe burst. Business investment soon followed, because there's no point in expanding capacity when sales are shrinking, and a lot of government spending has also fallen as local, state, and some national governments have found themselves starved for revenue. Low spending, in turn, means low employment, because businesses won't produce what they can't sell, and they won't hire workers if they don't need them for production. We are suffering from a severe overall lack of demand.

Attitudes toward what I just said vary widely. Some commentators consider it so obvious as not to be worth discussing. Others, however, regard it as nonsense. There are players on the political landscape—important players, with real influence—who don't believe that it's possible for the economy as a whole to suffer from inadequate demand. There can be lack of demand for some goods, they say, but there can't be too little demand across the board. Why? Because, they claim, people have to spend their income on *something*.

This is the fallacy Keynes called "Say's Law"; it's also sometimes called the "Treasury view," a reference not to our Treasury but to His Majesty's Treasury in the 1930s, an institution that insisted that any government spending would always displace an equal amount of private spending. Just so you know that I'm not describing a straw man, here's Brian Riedl of the Heritage Foundation (a right-wing think tank) in an early-2009 interview with *National Review*:

> The grand Keynesian myth is that you can spend money and thereby increase demand. And it's a myth because Congress does not have a vault of money to distribute in the economy. Every dollar Congress injects into the economy must first be taxed or borrowed *out of* the economy. You're not creating new demand, you're just transferring it from one group of people to another.

Give Riedl some credit: unlike many conservatives, he admits that his argument applies to any source of new spending. That is, he admits that his argument that a government spending program can't raise employment is also an argument that, say, a boom in business investment can't raise employment either. And it should apply to falling as well as rising spending. If, say, debt-burdened consumers choose to spend $500 billion less, that money, according to people like Riedl, must be going into banks, which will lend it out, so that businesses or other consumers will spend $500 billion more. If businesses afraid of that socialist in the White House scale back their investment spending, the money they thereby release must be spent by less nervous businesses or consumers. According to Riedl's logic, overall lack of demand can't hurt the economy, because it just can't happen.

Obviously I don't believe this, and in general sensible people don't. But how do we show that it's wrong? How can you convince people that it's wrong? Well, you can try to work through the logic verbally, but my experience is that when you try to have this kind of discussion with a determined anti-Keynesian, you end up caught in word games, with nobody persuaded. You can write down a little mathematical model to illustrate the issues, but this works only with economists, not with normal human beings (and it doesn't even work with some economists).

Or you can tell a true story—which brings me to my favorite economics story: the babysitting co-op.

The story was first told in a 1977 article in the *Journal of Money, Credit and Banking*, written by Joan and Richard Sweeney, who lived through the experience, and titled "Monetary Theory and the Great Capitol Hill Baby Sitting Co-op crisis." The Sweeneys were members of a babysitting co-op: an association of around 150 young couples, mainly congressional staffers, who saved money on babysitters by looking after each other's children.

The relatively large size of the co-op offered a big advantage, since the odds of finding someone able to do babysitting on a night you wanted to go out were good. But there was a problem: how could the co-op's founders ensure that each couple did its fair share of babysitting?

The co-op's answer was a scrip system: couples who joined the co-op were issued twenty coupons, each corresponding to one half hour of babysitting time. (Upon leaving the co-op, they were expected to give the same number of coupons back.) Whenever babysitting took place, the babysittees would give the babysitters the appropriate number of coupons. This ensured that over time each couple would do as much babysitting as it received, because coupons surrendered in return for services would have to be replaced.

Eventually, however, the co-op got into big trouble. On average, couples would try to keep a reserve of babysitting coupons in their desk drawers, just in case they needed to go out several times in a row. But for reasons not worth getting into, there came a point at which the number of babysitting coupons in circulation was substantially less than the reserve the average couple wanted to keep on hand.

So what happened? Couples, nervous about their low reserves of babysitting coupons, were reluctant to go out until they had increased their hoards by babysitting other couples' children. But precisely because many couples were reluctant to go out, opportunities to earn coupons through babysitting became scarce. This made coupon-poor couples even more reluctant to go out, and the volume of babysitting in the co-op fell sharply.

In short, the babysitting co-op fell into a depression, which lasted until the economists in the group managed to persuade the board to increase the supply of coupons.

What do we learn from this story? If you say "nothing," because it seems too cute and trivial, shame on you. The Capitol Hill babysitting co-op was a real, if miniature, monetary economy. It lacked many of the features of the enormous system we call the world economy, but it had one feature that is crucial to understanding what has gone wrong with that world economy—a feature that seems, time and again, to be beyond the ability of politicians and policy makers to grasp.

What is that feature? It is the fact that *your spending is my income, and my spending is your income.*

Isn't that obvious? Not to many influential people.

For example, it clearly wasn't obvious to John Boehner, the Speaker of the U.S. House, who opposed President Obama's economic plans, arguing that since Americans were suffering, it was time for the U.S. government to tighten its belt too. (To the great dismay of liberal economists, Obama ended up echoing that line in his own speeches.) The question Boehner didn't ask himself was, if ordinary citizens are tightening their belts—spending less—and the government also spends less, who is going to buy American products?

Similarly, the point that every individual's income—and every country's income, too—is someone else's spending is clearly not obvious to many German officials, who point to their country's turnaround between the late 1990s and today as a model for everyone else to follow. The key to that turnaround was a move on Germany's part from trade deficit to trade surplus—that is, from buying more from abroad than it sold abroad to the reverse. But that was possible only because other countries (mainly in southern Europe) correspondingly moved deep into trade deficit. Now we're all in trouble, but we can't all sell more than we buy. Yet the Germans don't seem to grasp that, perhaps because they don't want to.

And because the babysitting co-op, for all its simplicity and tiny scale, had this crucial, not at all obvious feature that's also true of the world economy, the co-op's experiences can serve as "proof of concept" for some important economic ideas. In this case, we learn at least three important lessons.

First, we learn that an overall inadequate level of demand is indeed a real possibility. When coupon-short members of the babysitting co-op decided to stop spending coupons on nights out, that decision didn't lead to any automatic offsetting rise in spending by other co-op members; on the contrary, the reduced availability of babysitting opportunities made everyone spend less. People like Brian Riedl are right that spending must always equal income: the number of babysitting coupons earned in a given week was always equal to the number of coupons spent. But this doesn't mean that people will always spend enough to make full use of the economy's productive capacity; it can instead mean that enough capacity stands idle to depress income *down* to the level of spending.

Second, an economy really can be depressed thanks to magneto trouble, that is, thanks to failures of coordination rather than lack of productive capacity. The co-op didn't get into trouble because its members were bad babysitters, or because high tax rates or too-generous government handouts made them unwilling to take babysitting jobs, or because they were paying the inevitable price for past excesses. It got into trouble for a seemingly trivial reason: the supply of coupons was too low, and this created a "colossal muddle," as Keynes put it, in which the members of the co-op were, as individuals, trying to do something—add to their hoards of coupons—that they could not, as a group, actually do.

This is a crucial insight. The current crisis in the global economy—an economy that's roughly 40 million times as large as the babysitting co-op—is, for all the differences in scale, very similar in character to the problems of the co-op. Collectively, the world's residents are trying to buy less stuff than they are capable of producing, to spend less than they earn. That's possible for an individual, but not for the world as a whole. And the result is the devastation all around us.

Let me say a bit more about that, offering a brief and simplified preview of the longer explanation to come. If we look at the state of the world on the eve of the crisis—say, in 2005–07—we see a picture in which some people were cheerfully lending a lot of money to other people, who were cheerfully spending that money. U.S. corporations were lending their excess cash to investment banks, which in turn were using the funds to finance home loans; German banks were lending excess cash to Spanish banks, which were also using the funds to finance home loans; and so on. Some of those loans were used to buy new houses, so that the funds ended up spent on construction. Some of the loans were used to extract money from home equity, which was used to buy consumer goods. And because your spending is my income, there were plenty of sales, and jobs were relatively easy to find.

Then the music stopped. Lenders became much more cautious about making new loans; the people who had been borrowing were forced to cut back sharply on their spending. And here's the problem: nobody else was ready to step up and spend in their place. Suddenly, total spending in the world economy plunged, and because my spending is your income and your spending is my income, incomes and employment plunged too.

So can anything be done? That's where we come to the third lesson from the babysitting co-op: big economic problems can sometimes have simple, easy solutions. The co-op got out of its mess simply by printing up more coupons.

This raises the key question: Could we cure the global slump the same way? Would printing more babysitting coupons, aka increasing the money supply, be all that it takes to get Americans back to work?

Well, the truth is that printing more babysitting coupons *is* the way we normally get out of recessions. For the last fifty years the business of ending recessions has basically been the job of the Federal Reserve, which (loosely speaking) controls the quantity of money circulating in the economy; when the economy turns down, the Fed cranks up the printing presses. And until now this has always worked. It worked spectacularly after the severe recession of 1981–82, which the Fed was able to turn within a few months into a rapid economic recovery—"morning in America." It worked, albeit more slowly and more hesitantly, after the 1990–91 and 2001 recessions.

But it didn't work this time around. I just said that the Fed "loosely speaking" controls the money supply; what it actually controls is the "monetary base," the sum of currency in circulation and reserves held by banks. Well, the Fed has tripled the size of the monetary base since 2008; yet the economy remains depressed. So is my argument that we're suffering from inadequate demand wrong?

No, it isn't. In fact, the failure of monetary policy to resolve this crisis was predictable—and predicted. I wrote the original version of my book *The Return of Depression Economics*, back in 1999, mainly to warn Americans that Japan had already found itself in a position where printing money couldn't revive its depressed economy, and that the same thing could happen to us. Back then a number of other economists shared my worries. Among them was none other than Ben Bernanke, now the Fed chairman.

So what did happen to us? We found ourselves in the unhappy condition known as a "liquidity trap."

The Liquidity Trap

In the middle years of the last decade, the U.S. economy was powered by two big things: lots of housing construction and strong consumer spending. Both of these things were, in turn, driven by high and rising housing prices, which led both to a building boom and to spending by consumers who felt rich. But the housing price rise was, it turns out, a bubble, based on unrealistic expectations. And when that bubble burst, it brought both construction and consumer spending down with it. In 2006, the peak of the bubble, builders broke ground for 1.8 million housing units; in 2010 they broke ground for only 585,000. In 2006 American consumers bought 16.5 million cars and light trucks; in 2010 they bought only 11.6 million. For about a year after the housing bubble popped, the U.S. economy kept its head above water by increasing exports, but by the end of 2007 it was headed down, and it has never really recovered.

The Federal Reserve, as I've already mentioned, responded by rapidly increasing the monetary base. Now, the Fed—unlike the board of the babysitting co-op—doesn't hand out coupons to families; when it wants to increase the money supply, it basically lends the funds to banks, hoping that the banks will lend those funds out in turn. (It usually buys bonds from banks rather than making direct loans, but it's more or less the same thing.)

This sounds very different from what the co-op did, but

the difference isn't actually very big. Remember, the rule of the co-op said that you had to return as many coupons when you left as you received on entering, so those coupons were in a way a loan from management. Increasing the supply of coupons therefore didn't make couples richer—they still had to do as much babysitting as they received. What it did, instead, was make them more *liquid*, increasing their ability to spend when they wanted without worrying about running out of funds.

Now, out in the non-babysitting world people and businesses can always add to their liquidity, but at a price: they can borrow cash, but have to pay interest on borrowed funds. What the Fed can do by pushing more cash into the banks is drive down interest rates, which are the price of liquidity—and also, of course, the price of borrowing to finance investment or other spending. So in the non-babysitting economy, the Fed's ability to drive the economy comes via its ability to move interest rates.

But here's the thing: it can push interest rates down only so far. Specifically, it can't push them below zero, because when rates get close to zero, just sitting on cash is a better option than lending money to other people. And in the current slump it didn't take long for the Fed to hit this "zero lower bound": it started cutting rates in late 2007 and had hit zero by late 2008. Unfortunately, a zero rate turned out not to be low enough, because the bursting of the housing bubble had done so much damage. Consumer spending remained weak; housing stayed flat on its back; business investment was low, because why expand without strong sales? And unemployment remained disastrously high.

And that's the liquidity trap: it's what happens when zero isn't low enough, when the Fed has saturated the economy with liquidity to such an extent that there's no cost to holding more cash, yet overall demand remains too low.

Let me go back to the babysitting co-op one last time, to provide what I hope is a helpful analogy. Suppose for some reason all, or at least most, of the co-op's members decided that they wanted to run a surplus this year, putting in more time minding other people's children than the amount of babysitting they received in return, so that they could do the reverse next year. In that case the co-op would have been in trouble no matter how many coupons the board issued. Any individual couple could accumulate coupons and save for next year; but the co-op as a whole couldn't, since babysitting time can't be stored. So there would have been a fundamental contradiction between what individual couples were trying to do and what was possible at the co-op-wide level: collectively, the co-op's members couldn't spend less than their income. Again, this comes back to the fundamental point that my spending is your income and your spending is my income. And the result of the attempt by individual couples to do what they could not, as a group, actually do would have been a depressed (and probably failed) co-op no matter how liberal the coupon policy.

That's more or less what has happened to America and the world economy as a whole. When everyone suddenly decided that debt levels were too high, debtors were forced to spend less, but creditors weren't willing to spend more, and the result has been a depression—not a Great Depression, but a depression all the same.

Yet surely there must be ways to fix this. It can't make sense for so much of the world's productive capacity to sit idle, for so many willing workers to be unable to find work. And yes, there are ways out. Before I get there, however, let's talk briefly about the views of those who don't believe any of what I've just said.

Is It Structural?

> *I believe this present labor supply of ours is peculiarly unadaptable and untrained. It cannot respond to the opportunities which industry may offer. This implies a situation of great inequality— full employment, much over-time, high wages, and great prosperity for certain favored groups, accompanied by low wages, short time, unemployment, and possibly destitution for others.*
>
> —Ewan Clague

The quotation above comes from an article in the *Journal of the American Statistical Association*. It makes an argument one hears from many quarters these days: that the fundamental problems we have run deeper than a mere lack of demand, that too many of our workers lack the skills the twenty-first-century economy requires, or too many of them are still stuck in the wrong locations or the wrong industry.

But I've just played a little trick on you: the article in question was published in 1935. The author was claiming that even if something were to lead to a great surge in the demand for American workers, unemployment would remain high, because those workers weren't up to the job. But he was completely wrong: when that surge in demand finally came, thanks to the military buildup that preceded America's entry into World War II, all those millions of unemployed workers proved perfectly capable of resuming a productive role.

Yet now, as then, there seems to be a strong urge—an urge not restricted to one side of the political divide—to see our problems as "structural," not easily resolved through an increase in demand. If we stay with the "magneto trouble" analogy, what many influential people argue is that replacing the battery won't work, because there must be big problems with the engine and the drive train too.

Sometimes this argument is presented in terms of a general lack of skills. For example, former president Bill Clinton (I told you this wasn't coming just from one side of the political divide) told the TV show *60 Minutes* that unemployment remained high "because people don't have the job skills for the jobs that are open." Sometimes it's framed in terms of a story about how technology is simply making workers unnecessary—which is what President Obama seemed to be saying when he told the *Today Show*,

> There are some structural issues with our economy where *a lot of businesses have learned to be much more efficient with fewer workers. You see it when you go to a bank and you use an ATM, you don't go to a bank teller.* Or you see it when you go to the airport and you use a kiosk instead of checking at the gate. [my emphasis]

And most common of all is the assertion that we can't expect a return to full employment anytime soon, because we need to transfer workers out of an overblown housing sector and retrain them for other jobs. Here's Charles Plosser, the president of the Federal Reserve Bank of Richmond, and an important voice arguing against policies to expand demand:

> *You can't change the carpenter into a nurse easily, and you can't change the mortgage broker into a computer expert in a manufacturing plant very easily.* Eventually that stuff will sort itself out. People will be retrained and they'll find jobs in other indus-

tries. *But monetary policy can't retrain people.* Monetary policy can't fix those problems. [my emphasis]

OK, how do we know that all of this is wrong?

Part of the answer is that Plosser's implicit picture of the unemployed—that the typical unemployed worker is someone who was in the construction sector, and hasn't adapted to the world after the housing bubble—is just wrong. Of the 13 million U.S. workers who were unemployed in October 2011, only 1.1 million (a mere 8 percent) had previously been employed in construction.

More broadly, if the problem is that many workers have the wrong skills, or are in the wrong place, those workers with the right skills in the right place should be doing well. They should be experiencing full employment and rising wages. So where are these people?

To be fair, there is full employment, even a labor shortage, on the High Plains: Nebraska and the Dakotas have low unemployment by historical standards, largely thanks to a surge in gas drilling. But those three states have a combined population only slightly larger than that of Brooklyn, and unemployment is high everywhere else.

And there are no major occupations or skill groups doing well. Between 2007 and 2010 unemployment roughly doubled in just about every category—blue-collar and white-collar, manufacturing and services, highly educated and uneducated. Nobody was getting big wage increases; in fact, as we saw in chapter 1, highly educated graduates were taking unusually large pay cuts, because they were forced to accept jobs that made no use of their education.

The bottom line is that if we had mass unemployment

because too many workers lacked the Right Stuff, we should be able to find a significant number of workers who *do* have that stuff prospering—and we can't. What we see instead is impoverishment all around, which is what happens when the economy suffers from inadequate demand.

So we have an economy crippled by lack of demand; the private sector, collectively, is trying to spend less than it earns, and the result is that income has fallen. Yet we're in a liquidity trap: the Fed can't persuade the private sector to spend more just by increasing the quantity of money in circulation. What is the solution? The answer is obvious; the problem is that so many influential people refuse to see that obvious answer.

Spending Our Way to Prosperity

In the middle of 1939 the U.S. economy was past the worst of the Great Depression, but the depression was by no means over. The government was not yet collecting comprehensive data on employment and unemployment, but as best we can tell the unemployment rate as we now define it was over 11 percent. That seemed to many people like a permanent state: the optimism of the early New Deal years had taken a hard blow in 1937, when the economy suffered a second severe recession.

Yet within two years the economy was booming, and unemployment was plunging. What happened?

The answer is that finally someone began spending enough to get the economy humming again. That "someone" was, of course, the government.

The object of that spending was basically destruction rather than construction; as the economists Robert Gordon and Robert Krenn put it, in the summer of 1940 the U.S. economy went to war. Long before Pearl Harbor, military spending soared as America rushed to replace the ships and other armaments sent to Britain as part of the lend-lease program, and as army camps were quickly built to house the millions of new recruits brought in by the draft. As military spending created jobs and family incomes rose, consumer spending also picked up (it would eventually be restrained by rationing, but that came later). As businesses saw their sales growing, they also responded by ramping up spending.

And just like that, the Depression was over, and all those "unadaptable and untrained" workers were back on the job.

Did it matter that the spending was for defense, not domestic programs? In economic terms, not at all: spending creates demand, whatever it's for. In political terms, of course, it mattered enormously: all through the Depression influential voices warned about the dangers of excessive government spending, and as a result the job-creation programs of the New Deal were always far too small, given the depth of the slump. What the threat of war did was to finally silence the voices of fiscal conservatism, opening the door for recovery—which is why I joked back in the summer of 2011 that what we really need right now is a fake threat of alien invasion that leads to massive spending on anti-alien defenses.

But the essential point is that what we need to get out of this current depression is another burst of government spending.

Is it really that simple? Would it really be that easy? Basically, yes. We do need to talk about the role of monetary policy, about implications for government debt, and about what must be done to ensure that the economy doesn't slide right back into depression when the government spending stops. We need to talk about ways to reduce the overhang of private debt that is arguably at the root of our slump. We also need

to talk about international aspects, especially the peculiar trap
Europe has created for itself. All of that will be covered later
in this book. But the core insight—that what the world needs
now is for governments to step up their spending to get us out
of this depression—will remain intact. Ending this depression
should be, could be, almost incredibly easy.

So why aren't we doing it? To answer that question, we
have to look at some economic and, even more important,
political history. First, however, let's talk some more about the
crisis of 2008, which plunged us into this depression.

CHAPTER THREE
THE MINSKY MOMENT

Once this massive credit crunch hit, it didn't take long before we were in a recession. The recession, in turn, deepened the credit crunch as demand and employment fell, and credit losses of financial institutions surged. Indeed, we have been in the grips of precisely this adverse feedback loop for more than a year. A process of balance sheet deleveraging has spread to nearly every corner of the economy. Consumers are pulling back on purchases, especially on durable goods, to build their savings. Businesses are cancelling planned investments and laying off workers to preserve cash. And, financial institutions are shrinking assets to bolster capital and improve their chances of weathering the current storm. Once again, Minsky understood this dynamic. He spoke of the paradox of deleveraging, in which precautions that may be smart for individuals and firms—and indeed essential to return the economy to a normal state—nevertheless magnify the distress of the economy as a whole.

—Janet Yellen, vice chair of the Federal Reserve,
from a speech titled "A Minksy Meltdown:
Lessons for Central Bankers," April 16, 2009

IN APRIL 2011 the Institute for New Economic Thinking— an organization founded in the wake of the 2008 financial crisis to promote, well, new economic thinking—held a conference in Bretton Woods, New Hampshire, site of a famous 1944 meeting that laid the foundations of the postwar world monetary system. One of the participants, Mark Thoma of the University of Oregon, who maintains the influential blog

Economist's View, cracked, after listening to some of the panels, that "new economic thinking means reading old books."

As others were quick to point out, he had a point, but there's a good reason why old books are back in vogue. Yes, economists have come up with some new ideas in the wake of the financial crisis. But arguably the most important change in thinking—at least among those economists who are at all willing to rethink their views in the light of the ongoing disaster, a smaller group than one might have hoped for—has been a renewed appreciation for the ideas of past economists. One of those past economists is, of course, John Maynard Keynes: we are recognizably living in the kind of world Keynes described. But two other dead economists have also made strong and justified comebacks: a contemporary of Keynes's, the American economist Irving Fisher, and a more recent entrant, the late Hyman Minsky. What's especially interesting about Minsky's new prominence is that he was very much out of the economic mainstream when he was alive. Why, then, are so many economists—including, as we saw at the beginning of this chapter, top officials at the Federal Reserve—now invoking his name?

The Night They Reread Minsky

Long before the crisis of 2008, Hyman Minsky was warning—to a largely indifferent economics profession—not just that something like that crisis could happen but that it *would* happen.

Few listened at the time. Minsky, who taught at Washington University in St. Louis, was a marginalized figure throughout his professional life, and died, still marginalized, in 1996. And to be honest, Minsky's heterodoxy wasn't the only reason he was ignored by the mainstream. His books are not, to say the least, user-friendly; nuggets of brilliant insight are strewn thinly across acres of turgid prose and unnecessary algebra. And he also cried wolf too often; to paraphrase an old joke by Paul Samuelson, he predicted around nine of the last three major financial crises.

Yet these days many economists, yours truly very much included, recognize the importance of Minsky's "financial instability hypothesis." And those of us, again like yours truly, who were relative latecomers to Minsky's work wish that we had read it much earlier.

Minsky's big idea was to focus on leverage—on the buildup of debt relative to assets or income. Periods of economic stability, he argued, lead to rising leverage, because everyone becomes complacent about the risk that borrowers might not be able to repay. But this rise in leverage eventually leads to economic instability. Indeed, it prepares the ground for financial and economic crisis.

Let's take this in stages.

First of all, debt is a very useful thing. We'd be a poorer society if everyone who wanted to purchase a home had to pay in cash, if every small-business owner seeking to expand either had to pay for that expansion out of his or her own pocket or take on extra, unwanted partners. Debt is a way for those without good uses for their money right now to put that money to work, for a price, in the service of those who do have good uses for it.

Also, contrary to what you might think, debt does not make society as a whole poorer: one person's debt is another person's asset, so total wealth is unaffected by the amount of debt out there. This is, strictly speaking, true only for the world economy as a whole, not for any one country, and there are countries whose foreign liabilities are much bigger than their overseas assets. But despite all you may have heard about borrowing from China and all that, this isn't true of the United States: our "net international investment position," the difference between our overseas assets and our overseas liabilities, is in the red "only" to the tune of $2.5 trillion. That sounds like a lot, but it's actually not much in the context of an economy that produces $15 trillion worth of goods and services every year. There has been a rapid increase in U.S. debt since 1980, but that rapid rise in debt didn't put us deeply in hock to the rest of the world.

It did, however, make us vulnerable to the kind of crisis that struck in 2008.

Obviously, being highly leveraged—having a lot of debt relative to your income or assets—makes you vulnerable when things go wrong. A family that bought its house with no money down and an interest-only mortgage is going to find itself underwater and in trouble if the housing market turns down, even a bit; a family that put 20 percent down and has been paying off principal ever since is a lot more likely to weather a downturn. A company obliged to devote most of its cash flow to paying off debt incurred from a leveraged buyout may go under quickly if sales falter, while a debt-free business may be able to ride out the storm.

What may be less obvious is that when many people and businesses are highly leveraged, the economy as a whole becomes vulnerable when things go wrong. For high levels of debt leave the economy vulnerable to a sort of death spiral in which the very efforts of debtors to "deleverage," to reduce their debt, create an environment that makes their debt problems even worse.

The great American economist Irving Fisher laid out the

story in a classic 1933 article titled "The Debt-Deflation Theory of Great Depressions"—an article that, like the Keynes
essay with which I opened chapter 2, reads, stylistic archaisms aside, as if it had been written just the other day. Imagine, said Fisher, that an economic downturn creates a situation
in which many debtors find themselves forced to take quick
action to reduce their debt. They can "liquidate," that is, try to
sell whatever assets they have, and/or they can slash spending
and use their income to pay down their debts. Those measures
can work if not too many people and businesses are trying to
pay down debt at the same time.

But if too many players in the economy find themselves
in debt trouble at the same time, their collective efforts to get
out of that trouble are self-defeating. If millions of troubled
homeowners try to sell their houses to pay off their mortgages—or, for that matter, if their homes are seized by creditors, who then try to sell the foreclosed properties—the result
is plunging home prices, which puts even more homeowners
underwater and leads to even more forced sales. If banks worry
about the amount of Spanish and Italian debt on their books,
and decide to reduce their exposure by selling off some of that
debt, the prices of Spanish and Italian bonds plunge—and that
endangers the stability of the banks, forcing them to sell even
more assets. If consumers slash spending in an effort to pay off
their credit card debt, the economy slumps, jobs disappear, and
the burden of consumer debt gets even worse. And if things
get bad enough, the economy as a whole can suffer from deflation—falling prices across the board—which means that the
purchasing power of the dollar rises, and hence that the *real*
burden of debt rises even if the dollar value of debts is falling.

Irving Fisher summed it up with a pithy slogan that was a bit imprecise, but gets at the essential truth: *The more the debtors pay, the more they owe.* He argued that this was the real story behind the Great Depression—that the U.S. economy came into a recession with an unprecedented level of debt that made it vulnerable to a self-reinforcing downward spiral. He was almost surely right. And as I've already said, his article reads as if had been written yesterday; that is, a similar if less extreme story is the main explanation of the depression we're in right now.

The Minsky Moment

Let me try to match Fisher's pithy slogan about debt deflation with a similarly imprecise, but I hope evocative, slogan about the current state of the world economy: right now, *debtors can't spend, and creditors won't spend.*

You can see this dynamic very clearly if you look at European governments. Europe's debtor nations, the countries like Greece and Spain that borrowed a lot of money during the good years before the crisis (mostly to finance private spending, not government spending, but leave that aside for now), are all facing fiscal crises: they either can't borrow money at all, or can do so only at extremely high interest rates. They have so far managed to avoid literally running out of cash, because in a variety of ways stronger European economies like Germany and the European Central Bank have been funneling loans in their direction. This aid has, however, come with strings attached: the debtor countries' governments have been forced to impose savage austerity programs, slashing spending even on basic items like health care.

Yet creditor countries aren't engaged in any offsetting spending increases. In fact, they, too, worried about the risks of debt, are engaged in austerity programs, albeit milder than those in the debtors.

That's a story about European governments; but a similar dynamic is playing out in the private sector, both in Europe and in the United States. Look, for example, at spending by U.S. households. We can't directly track how households with different levels of debt have changed their spending, but as the economists Atif Mian and Amir Sufi have pointed out, we do have county-level data on debt and spending on items like houses and cars—and debt levels vary a lot across U.S. counties. Sure enough, what Mian and Sufi find is that counties with high levels of debt have cut back drastically on both auto sales and home construction, while those with low debt have not; but the low-debt counties are buying only about as much as they were before the crisis, so there has a been a large fall in overall demand.

The consequence of this fall in overall demand is, as we saw in chapter 2, a depressed economy and high unemployment.

But why is this happening now, as opposed to five or six years ago? And how did debtors get that deep into debt in the first place? That's where Hyman Minsky comes in.

As Minsky pointed out, leverage—rising debt compared with income or assets—feels good until it feels terrible. In an expanding economy with rising prices, especially prices of assets like houses, borrowers are generally winners. You buy a house with almost no money down, and a few years later you have a substantial equity stake, simply because home prices have risen. A speculator buys stocks on margin, stock prices rise, and the more he borrowed the bigger his profit.

But why are lenders willing to allow this borrowing? Because as long as the economy as a whole is doing fairly well, debt doesn't seem very risky. Take the case of home mortgages. A few years ago researchers at the Federal Reserve Bank of Boston looked at the determinants of mortgage defaults, in which borrowers can't or won't pay. They found that as long as home prices were rising, even borrowers who had lost their jobs rarely defaulted; they just sold their houses and paid off their debts. Similar stories apply to many kinds of borrowers. As long as nothing very bad happens to the economy, lending doesn't seem very risky.

And here's the thing: as long as debt levels are fairly low, bad economic events are likely to be few and far between. So an economy with low debt tends to be an economy in which debt looks safe, an economy in which the memory of the bad things debt can do fades into the mists of history. Over time, the perception that debt is safe leads to more relaxed lending standards; businesses and families alike develop the habit of borrowing; and the overall level of leverage in the economy rises.

All of which, of course, sets the stage for future catastrophe. At some point there is a "Minsky moment," a phrase coined by the economist Paul McCulley of the bond fund Pimco. This moment is also sometimes known as a Wile E. Coyote moment, after the cartoon character known for running off cliffs, then hanging suspended in midair until he looks down—for only then, according to the laws of cartoon physics, does he plunge.

Once debt levels are high enough, anything can trigger the Minsky moment—a run-of-the-mill recession, the popping of a housing bubble, and so on. The immediate cause hardly matters; the important thing is that lenders rediscover the risks of debt, debtors are forced to start deleveraging, and Fisher's debt-deflation spiral begins.

Now let's look at some numbers. The figure on page 49 shows household debt as a percentage of GDP. I divide by GDP, the total income earned in the economy, because that corrects both for inflation and for economic growth; household debt in 1955 was about four times as high in dollar terms as in 1929, but thanks to inflation and growth it was much smaller in economic terms.

The Fall and Rise of Household Debt

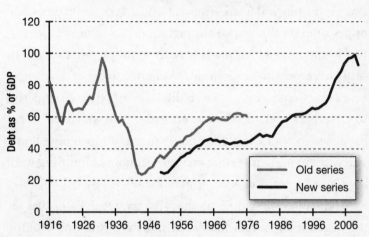

U.S. households reduced their debt burden during World War II, setting the stage for prosperity, but debt levels soared again after 1980, laying the foundations for our current depression.

Source: *Historical Statistics of the United States*, millennial ed. (Oxford University Press), and Federal Reserve Board

Also, notice that the data aren't fully compatible over time. One set of data runs from 1916 to 1976; another set, which for technical reasons shows a somewhat lower number, runs from 1950 up to the present. I've shown both series, including the overlap, which I think is enough to convey an overall sense of the long-run story.

And what a story it is! That huge run-up in the debt/ GDP ratio between 1929 and 1933 is Fisher's debt deflation in action: debt wasn't soaring, GDP was plunging, as the efforts of debtors to reduce their debt caused a combination of depression and deflation that made their debt problems even worse. Recovery under the New Deal, imperfect as it was, brought the debt ratio roughly back down to where it started.

Then came World War II. During the war the private sector was pretty much denied any new loans, even as incomes and prices rose. At the war's end, private debt was very low relative to income, which made it possible for private demand to surge once wartime rationing and controls were ended. Many economists (and quite a few businessmen) expected America to slide back into depression once the war was over. What happened instead was a great boom in private spending, home purchases in particular, that kept the economy humming until the Great Depression was a distant memory.

And it was the fading memory of the Depression that set the stage for an extraordinary rise in debt, beginning roughly in 1980. And yes, that coincided with the election of Ronald Reagan, because part of the story is political. Debt began rising in part because lenders and borrowers had forgotten that bad things can happen, but it also rose because politicians and supposed experts alike had forgotten that bad things can happen, and started to remove the regulations introduced in the 1930s to stop them from happening again.

Then, of course, the bad things did indeed happen again. The result was not simply to create an economic crisis but to create a special kind of economic crisis, one in which seemingly sensible policy responses are often exactly the wrong thing to do.

Looking-Glass Economics

If you spend a fair bit of time listening to what seemingly serious people say about the current state of the economy—and my job as pundit means that I do just that—you eventually recognize one of their biggest problems: they're working with the wrong metaphors. They think of the U.S. economy as if it were a family fallen on hard times, its income reduced by forces beyond its control, burdened with a debt too large for its income. And what they prescribe to remedy this situation is a regime of virtue and prudence: we must tighten our belts, reduce our spending, pay down our debts, cut our costs.

But this isn't that kind of crisis. Our income is down precisely because we are spending too little, and cutting our spending further will only depress our income even more. We do have a problem of excess debt, but that debt isn't money owed to some outsider; it's money we owe to one another, which makes a huge difference. And as for cutting costs: cutting costs compared to whom? If everyone tries to cut costs, it will only make things worse.

We are, in short, temporarily on the other side of the looking glass. The combination of the liquidity trap—even a zero interest rate isn't low enough to restore full employment—and the overhang of excessive debt has landed us in a world of paradoxes, a world in which virtue is vice and prudence is folly, and most of the things serious people demand that we do actually make our situation worse.

What are the paradoxes of which I speak? One of them, the "paradox of thrift," used to be widely taught in introductory economics, although it became less fashionable as the memory of the Great Depression faded. It goes like this: suppose everyone tries to save more at the same time. You might think that this increased desire to save would get translated into higher investment—more spending on new factories, office buildings, shopping malls, and so on—which would enhance our future wealth. But in a depressed economy, all that happens when everyone tries to save more (and therefore spends less) is that income declines and the economy shrinks. And as the economy becomes even more depressed, businesses will invest less, not more: in attempting to save more as individuals, consumers end up saving less in aggregate.

The paradox of thrift, as usually stated, doesn't necessarily depend on a legacy of excessive borrowing in the past, although that's in practice how we end up with a persistently depressed economy. But the overhang of debt causes two additional, related paradoxes.

First is the "paradox of deleveraging," which we've already seen summed up in Fisher's pithy slogan that the more debtors pay, the more they owe. A world in which a large fraction of individuals and/or companies is trying to pay down debt, all at once, is a world of falling income and asset values, in which debt problems become worse rather than better.

Second is the "paradox of flexibility." This is more or less implied by Fisher's old essay, but its modern incarnation, as far as I know, comes from the economist Gauti Eggertsson at the New York Fed. It goes like this: ordinarily, when you're having trouble selling something, the solution is to cut the price. So it seems natural to suppose that the solution to mass unemployment is to cut wages. In fact, conservative economists often argue that FDR delayed recovery in the 1930s, because the New Deal's prolabor policies raised wages when they should have been falling. And today it's often argued that more labor market "flexibility"—a euphemism for wage cuts—is what we really need.

But while an individual worker can improve his chances of getting a job by accepting a lower wage, because that makes him more attractive compared with other workers, an across-the-board cut in wages leaves everyone in the same place, except for one thing: it reduces everyone's income, but the level of debt remains the same. So more flexibility in wages (and prices) would just make matters worse.

Now, some readers may already have had a thought: if I've just explained why doing things that are normally considered virtuous and prudent makes us worse off in the current situation, doesn't that mean that we should in fact be doing the opposite of those things? And the answer, basically, is yes. At a time when many debtors are trying to save more and pay down debt, it's important that *someone* do the opposite, spending more and borrowing—with the obvious someone being the government. So this is just another way of arriving at the Keynesian argument for government spending as a necessary answer to the kind of depression we find ourselves facing.

What about the argument that falling wages and prices make the situation worse; does that mean that rising wages and prices would make things better, that inflation would actually be helpful? Yes, it does, because inflation would reduce the burden of debt (as well as having some other useful effects, which we'll talk about later). More broadly, policies to reduce the burden of debt one way or another, such as mortgage relief, could and should be a part of achieving a lasting exit from depression.

But that's getting ahead of ourselves. Before taking on the full outlines of a recovery strategy, I want to spend the next few chapters delving more deeply into how we got into this depression in the first place.

CHAPTER FOUR

BANKERS GONE WILD

[R]ecent regulatory reform, coupled with innovative technologies, has stimulated the development of financial products, such as asset-backed securities, collateral loan obligations, and credit default swaps, that facilitate the dispersion of risk. . . .

These increasingly complex financial instruments have contributed to the development of a far more flexible, efficient, and hence resilient financial system than the one that existed just a quarter-century ago.

—Alan Greenspan, October 12, 2005

IN 2005 ALAN GREENSPAN was still regarded as the Maestro, a source of oracular economic wisdom. And his comments about how the wonders of modern finance had ushered in a new age of stability were taken to reflect that oracular wisdom. The wizards of Wall Street, said Greenspan, had ensured that nothing like the great financial disruptions of the past could happen again.

Reading those words now, one is struck by how perfectly Greenspan got it wrong. The financial innovations he identified as sources of improved financial stability were precisely—*precisely*—what brought the financial system to the brink of collapse less than three years later. We now know that the sale of "asset-backed securities"—basically, the ability of banks to sell bunches of mortgages and other loans to poorly informed investors, instead of keeping them on their own books—encouraged reckless lending. Collateralized loan obligations—created by slicing, dicing, and pureeing bad debt—initially received AAA ratings, again sucking in gullible investors, but as soon as things went bad, these assets came to be known, routinely, as "toxic waste." And credit default swaps helped banks pretend that their investments were safe because someone else had insured them against losses; when things went wrong, it became obvious that the insurers, AIG in particular, didn't have anything like enough money to make good on their promises.

The thing is, Greenspan wasn't alone in his delusions. On the eve of the financial crisis, discussion of the financial system, both in the United States and in Europe, was marked by extraordinary complacency. Those few economists who worried about rising levels of debt and an increasingly casual attitude toward risk were marginalized, if not ridiculed.

And this marginalization was reflected both in private-sector behavior and in public policy: step by step, the rules and regulations that had been put in place in the 1930s to protect against banking crises were dismantled.

Bankers Unbound

I don't know what the government is coming to. Instead of protecting businessmen, it pokes its nose into business! Why, they're even talking now about having bank examiners. As if we bankers don't know how to run our own banks! Why, at home I have a letter from a popinjay official saying they were going to inspect my books. I have a slogan that should be blazoned on every newspaper in this country: America for the Americans! The government must not

*interfere with business! Reduce taxes! Our national debt is some-
thing shocking. Over one billion dollars a year! What this country
needs is a businessman for president!*

—Gatewood, the banker in *Stagecoach* (1939)

Like the other lines I've been pulling from the 1930s, the banker's rant from John Ford's classic film *Stagecoach* sounds—the
bit about "popinjays" aside—as if it could have been delivered
yesterday. What you need to know, if you've never seen the
movie (which you should), is that Gatewood is in fact a crook.
The reason he's on that stagecoach is that he has embezzled all
the funds in his bank and is skipping town.

Clearly, John Ford didn't have a particularly high opinion
of bankers. But then, in 1939 nobody did. The experiences of
the past decade, and in particular the wave of bank failures that
swept America in 1930–31, had created both broad distrust
and a demand for tighter regulation. Some of the regulations
imposed in the 1930s remain in place to this day, which is why
there haven't been many traditional bank runs in this crisis.
Others, however, were dismantled in the 1980s and 1990s.
Equally important, the regulations weren't updated to deal
with a changing financial system. This combination of deregulation and failure to keep regulations updated was a big factor
in the debt surge and the crisis that followed.

Let's start by talking about what banks do, and why they
need to be regulated.

Banking as we know it actually began almost by acci-
dent, as a sideline of a very different business, goldsmithing.
Goldsmiths, by virtue of the high value of their raw material,
always had really strong, theft-resistant safes. Some of them
began renting out the use of these safes: individuals who had
gold but no safe place to keep it would put it in the goldsmiths'

care, receiving a ticket that would allow them to claim their gold whenever they wanted it.

At this point two interesting things started happening. First, the goldsmiths discovered that they didn't really have to keep all that gold in their safes. Since it was unlikely that all the people who had deposited gold with them would demand it at the same time, it was (usually) safe to lend much of the gold out, keeping only a fraction in reserve. Second, tickets for stored gold began circulating as a form of currency; instead of paying someone with actual gold coins, you could transfer ownership of some of the coins you had stored with a goldsmith, so the slip of paper corresponding to those coins became, in a sense, as good as gold.

And that's what banking is all about. Investors generally face a trade-off between *liquidity*—the ability to lay your hands on funds on short notice—and *returns*, putting your money to work earning even more money. Cash in your pocket is perfectly liquid, but earns no return; an investment in, say, a promising start-up may pay off handsomely if all goes well, but can't easily be turned into cash if you face some financial emergency. What banks do is partially remove the need for this trade-off. A bank provides its depositors with liquidity, since they can lay hands on their funds whenever they want. Yet it puts most of those funds to work earning returns in longer-term investments, such as business loans or home mortgages.

So far, so good—and banking is a very good thing, not just for bankers but for the economy as a whole, most of the time. On occasion, however, banking can go very wrong, for the whole structure depends on depositors' not all wanting their funds at the same time. If for some reason all or at least many of a bank's depositors *do* decide simultaneously to withdraw their funds, the bank will be in big trouble: it doesn't have the cash on hand, and if it tries to raise cash quickly by selling off loans and other assets, it will have to offer fire-sale prices—and quite possibly go bankrupt in the process.

What would lead many of a bank's depositors to try withdrawing their funds at the same time? Why, fear that the bank might be about to fail, perhaps because so many depositors are trying to get out.

So banking carries with it, as an inevitable feature, the possibility of bank runs—sudden losses of confidence that cause panics, which end up becoming self-fulfilling prophecies. Furthermore, bank runs can be contagious, both because panic may spread to other banks and because one bank's fire sales, by driving down the value of other banks' assets, can push those other banks into the same kind of financial distress.

As some readers may already have noticed, there's a clear family resemblance between the logic of bank runs—especially contagious bank runs—and that of the Minsky moment, in which everyone simultaneously tries to pay down debt. The main difference is that high levels of debt and leverage in the economy as a whole, making a Minsky moment possible, happen only occasionally, whereas banks are *normally* leveraged enough that a sudden loss of confidence can become a self-fulfilling prophecy. The possibility of bank runs is more or less inherent in the nature of banking.

Before the 1930s there were two main answers to the problem of bank runs. First, banks themselves tried to seem as solid as possible, both through appearances—that's why bank buildings were so often massive marble structures—and by actually being very cautious. In the nineteenth century banks often had "capital ratios" of 20 or 25 percent—that is, the value of their deposits was only 75 or 80 percent of the value of their assets. This meant that a nineteenth-century bank could lose as much as 20 or 25 percent of the money it had lent out, and still be able to pay off its depositors in full. By contrast, many financial institutions on the eve of the 2008 crisis had capital backing only a few percent of their assets, so that even small losses could "break the bank."

Second, there were efforts to create "lenders of last resort"—institutions that could advance funds to banks in a panic, and thereby ensure that depositors were paid and the panic subsided. In Britain, the Bank of England began playing that role early in the nineteenth century. In the United States, the Panic of 1907 was met with an ad hoc response organized by J. P. Morgan, and the realization that you couldn't always count on having J. P. Morgan around led to the creation of the Federal Reserve.

But these traditional responses proved dramatically inadequate in the 1930s, so Congress stepped in. The Glass–Steagall Act of 1933 (and similar legislation in other countries) established what amounted to a system of levees to protect the economy against financial floods. And for about half a century, that system worked pretty well.

On one side, Glass–Steagall established the Federal Deposit Insurance Corporation (FDIC), which guaranteed (and still guarantees) depositors against loss if their bank should happen to fail. If you've ever seen the movie *It's a Wonderful Life*, which features a run on Jimmy Stewart's bank, you might be interested to know that the scene is completely anachronistic: by the time the supposed bank run takes place, that is, just after World War II, deposits were already insured, and old-fashioned bank runs were things of the past.

On the other side, Glass-Steagall limited the amount of risk banks could take. This was especially necessary given the establishment of deposit insurance, which could have created enormous "moral hazard." That is, it could have created a situation in which bankers could raise lots of money, no questions asked—hey, it's all government-insured—then put that money into high-risk, high-stakes investments, figuring that it was heads they win, tails taxpayers lose. One of the first of many deregulatory disasters came in the 1980s, when savings and loan institutions demonstrated, with a vengeance, that this kind of taxpayer-subsidized gambling was more than a theoretical possibility.

So banks were subjected to a number of rules intended to prevent them from gambling with depositors' funds. Most notably, any bank accepting deposits was restricted to the business of making loans; you couldn't use depositors' funds to speculate in stock markets or commodities, and in fact you couldn't house such speculative activities under the same institutional roof. The law therefore sharply separated ordinary banking, the sort of thing done by the likes of Chase Manhattan, from "investment banking," the sort of thing done by the likes of Goldman Sachs.

Thanks to deposit insurance, as I've said, the old-fashioned bank run became a thing of the past. And thanks to regulation, banks grew much more cautious about lending than they had been before the Great Depression. The result was what Yale's Gary Gorton calls the "quiet period," a long era of relative stability and absence of financial crises.

All that began to change, however, in 1980.

In that year, of course, Ronald Reagan was elected president, signaling a dramatic rightward turn in American politics.

But in a way Reagan's election only formalized a sea change in attitudes toward government intervention that was well under way even during the Carter administration. Carter presided over the deregulation of airlines, which transformed the way Americans traveled, the deregulation of trucking, which transformed the distribution of goods, and the deregulation of oil and natural gas. These measures, by the way, met with near-universal approval on the part of economists, then and now: there really wasn't and isn't a good reason for the government to be setting air fares or trucking rates, and increased competition in these industries led to widespread efficiency gains.

Given the spirit of the times, it probably shouldn't be surprising that finance was also subject to deregulation. One major step in that direction also took place under Carter, who passed the Monetary Control Act of 1980, which ended regulations that had prevented banks from paying interest on many kinds of deposits. Reagan followed up with the Garn–St. Germain Act of 1982, which relaxed restrictions on the kinds of loans banks could make.

Unfortunately, banking is not like trucking, and the effect of deregulation was not so much to encourage efficiency as to encourage risk taking. Letting banks compete by offering interest on deposits sounded like a good deal for consumers. But it increasingly turned banking into a case of survival of the most reckless, in which only those who were willing to make dubious loans could afford to pay depositors a competitive rate. Removing restrictions on the interest rates that banks could charge made reckless loans more attractive, since bankers could lend to customers who promised to pay a lot—but might not honor their promises. The scope for high rolling was further increased when rules that had limited

exposure to particular lines of business, or to individual borrowers, were loosened.

These changes led to a sharp rise in lending and in the
riskiness of lending, as well as, just a few years later, some
big banking problems—exacerbated by the way some banks
financed their lending by borrowing money from other banks.

Nor did the trend of deregulation end with Reagan. One
more big loosening of the rules occurred under the next
Democratic president: Bill Clinton dealt the final blow to—
Depression-era regulation, by lifting the Glass-Steagall rules
that had separated commercial and investment banking.

Arguably, however, these changes in regulation were
less important than what *didn't* change—regulations weren't
updated to reflect the changing nature of banking.

What, after all, is a bank? Traditionally a bank has meant
a depository institution, a place where you deposit money at
a window and can withdraw it at will from that same window. But as far as the economics are concerned, a bank is any
institution that borrows short and lends long, that promises
people easy access to their funds, even as it uses most of those
funds to make investments that can't be converted into cash
at short notice. Depository institutions—big marble buildings
with rows of tellers—are the traditional way to pull this off.
But there are other ways to do it.

One obvious example is money market funds, which don't
have a physical presence like banks and don't provide literal
cash (green pieces of paper bearing portraits of dead presidents), but otherwise function a lot like checking accounts.
Businesses looking for a place to park their cash often turn
to "repo," in which borrowers like Lehman Brothers borrow
money for very short periods—often just overnight—using
assets like mortgage-backed securities as collateral; they use

the money thus raised to buy even more of these assets. And there are other arrangements, like "auction rate securities" (don't ask), that once again serve much the same purposes as ordinary banking, without being subject to the rules that govern conventional banking.

This set of alternative ways to do what banks do has come to be known as "shadow banking." Thirty years ago, shadow banking was a minor part of the financial system; banking really was about big marble buildings with rows of tellers. By 2007, however, shadow banking was bigger than old-fashioned banking.

What became clear in 2008—and should have been realized much earlier—was that shadow banks pose the same risks as conventional banks. Like depository institutions, they are highly leveraged; like conventional banks, they can be brought down by self-fulfilling panics. So as shadow banking rose in importance, it should have been subjected to regulations similar to those covering traditional banks.

But given the political temper of the times, that wasn't going to happen. Shadow banking was allowed to grow without policing—and it grew all the faster precisely because shadow banks were allowed to take bigger risks than conventional banks.

Not surprisingly, the conventional banks wanted in on the action, and in an increasingly money-dominated political system, they got what they wanted. Glass-Steagall's enforced separation between depository banking and investment banking was repealed in 1999 at the specific urging of Citicorp, the holding company of Citibank, which wanted to merge with Travelers Group, a firm that engaged in investment banking, to become Citigroup.

The result was an increasingly unregulated system in which banks were free to give in fully to the overconfidence that the quiet period had created. Debt soared, risks multiplied, and the foundations for crisis were laid.

The Big Lie

> *I hear your complaints. Some of them are totally unfounded. It was not the banks that created the mortgage crisis. It was, plain and simple, Congress who forced everybody to go and give mortgages to people who were on the cusp. Now, I'm not saying I'm sure that was terrible policy, because a lot of those people who got homes still have them and they wouldn't have gotten them without that.*
>
> *But they were the ones who pushed Fannie and Freddie to make a bunch of loans that were imprudent, if you will. They were the ones that pushed the banks to loan to everybody. And now we want to go vilify the banks because it's one target, it's easy to blame them and congress certainly isn't going to blame themselves. At the same time, Congress is trying to pressure banks to loosen their lending standards to make more loans. This is exactly the same speech they criticized them for.*
>
> —Michael Bloomberg, mayor of New York,
> on the Occupy Wall Street protests

The story I have just told about complacency and deregulation is, in fact, what happened in the run-up to crisis. But you may have heard a different story—the one told by Michael Bloomberg in the quotation above. According to this story, debt growth was caused by liberal do-gooders and government agencies, which forced banks to lend to minority home buyers and subsidized dubious mortgages. This alternative story, which says that it's all the government's fault, is dogma on the right. From the point of view of most, indeed virtually all, Republicans, it's an unquestioned truth.

It isn't true, of course. The fund manager and blogger Barry Ritholtz, who isn't especially political but has a keen eye for flimflam, calls it the Big Lie of the financial crisis.

How do we know that the Big Lie is, in fact, not true? There are two main kinds of evidence.

First, any explanation that blames the U.S. Congress, with its supposed desire to see low-income families own homes, for the explosion of credit must confront the awkward fact that the credit boom and the housing bubble were very widespread, including many markets and assets that had nothing to do with low-income borrowers. There were housing bubbles and credit booms in Europe; there was a price surge, followed by defaults and losses after the bubble popped, in commercial real estate; within the United States, the biggest booms and busts weren't in inner-city areas but rather in suburbs and exurbs.

Second, the great bulk of risky lending was undertaken by private lenders—and loosely regulated private lenders, at that. In particular, subprime loans—mortgage loans to borrowers who didn't qualify according to normal prudential standards—were overwhelmingly made by private firms that were neither covered by the Community Reinvestment Act, which was supposed to encourage loans to members of minority groups, nor supervised by Fannie Mae and Freddie Mac, the government-sponsored agencies charged with encouraging home lending. In fact, during most of the housing bubble Fannie and Freddie were rapidly losing market share, because private lenders would take on borrowers the government-sponsored agencies wouldn't. Freddie Mac did start buying subprime mortgages from loan originators late in the game, but it was clearly a follower, not a leader.

In an attempt to refute this latter point, analysts at right-wing think tanks—notably Edward Pinto at the American Enterprise Institute—have produced data showing Fannie and Freddie underwriting a lot of "subprime and other high-risk" mortgages, lumping loans to borrowers without stellar credit scores in with loans to borrowers who failed strict lending criteria in other ways. This leads readers who don't know better to think that Fannie and Freddie were actually deeply involved in promoting subprime lending. But they weren't, and the "other high-risk" stuff turns out, on examination, to have been not especially high-risk, with default rates far below those on subprime loans.

I could go on, but you get the point. The attempt to blame government for the financial crisis falls apart in the face of even a cursory look at the facts, and the attempts to get around those facts smack of deliberate deception. This raises a question: why do conservatives want so badly to believe, and to get other people to believe, that the government did it?

The immediate answer is obvious: to believe anything else would be to admit that your political movement has been on the wrong track for decades. Modern conservatism is dedicated to the proposition that unfettered markets and the unrestricted pursuit of profit and personal gain are the keys to prosperity—and that the much-expanded role for government that emerged from the Great Depression did nothing but harm. Yet what we actually see is a story in which conservatives gained power, set about dismantling many of those Depression-era protections—and the economy plunged into a second depression, not as bad as the first, but bad enough. Conservatives badly need to explain this awkward history away, to tell a story that makes government, not lack of government, the villain.

But this in a way only pushes the question back a step. How did conservative ideology, the belief that government is always the problem, never the solution, come to have such a firm grip on our political discourse? That's a slightly harder question to answer than you might think.

The Not-So-Good Years

From what I've said so far, you might think that the story of the U.S. economy since around 1980 was one of illusory prosperity, of what felt like good times, until the debt bubble burst in 2008. And there's something to that. Yet it's a story that needs qualifying, because the truth is that even the good times weren't all that good, in a couple of ways.

First, even though the United States avoided a debilitating financial crisis until 2008, the dangers of a deregulated banking system were becoming apparent much earlier for those willing to see.

In fact, deregulation created a serious disaster almost immediately. In 1982, as I've already mentioned, Congress passed, and Ronald Reagan signed, the Garn–St. Germain Act, which Reagan described at the signing ceremony as "the first step in our administration's comprehensive program of financial deregulation." Its principal purpose was to help solve the problems of the thrift (savings and loan) industry, which had gotten into trouble after inflation rose in the 1970s. Higher inflation led to higher interest rates and left thrifts—which had lent lots of money long-term at low rates—in a troubled position. A number of thrifts were at risk of failing; since their deposits were federally insured, many of their losses would ultimately fall on taxpayers.

Yet politicians were unwilling to bite that bullet and looked for a way out. At that signing ceremony, Reagan explained how it was supposed to work:

What this legislation does is expand the powers of thrift institutions by permitting the industry to make commercial loans and increase their consumer lending. It reduces their exposure to changes in the housing market and in interest rate levels. This in turn will make the thrift industry a stronger, more effective force in financing housing for millions of Americans in the years to come.

But it didn't work out that way. What happened instead was that deregulation created a classic case of moral hazard, in which the owners of thrifts had every incentive to engage in highly risky behavior. After all, depositors didn't care what their bank did; they were insured against losses. So the smart move for a banker was to make high-interest-rate loans to dubious borrowers, typically real estate developers. If things went well, the bank would register large profits. If they went badly, the banker could just walk away. It was heads he won, tails the taxpayers lost.

Oh, and loose regulation also created a permissive environment for outright theft, in which loans were made to friends and relatives, who disappeared with the money. Remember Gatewood, the banker in *Stagecoach*? There were a lot of Gatewoods in the thrift industry of the 1980s.

By 1989 it was obvious that the thrift industry had run wild, and the feds finally shut down the casino. By that time, however, the industry's losses had ballooned. In the end, taxpayers faced a bill of about $130 billion. That was serious money at the time—relative to the size of the economy, it was the equivalent of more than $300 billion today.

Nor was the savings and loan mess the only signal that deregulation was more dangerous than its advocates let on. In the early 1990s there were major problems at big commercial banks, Citi in particular, because they had overextended themselves in lending to commercial real estate developers.

In 1998, with much of the emerging world in financial crisis, the failure of a single hedge fund, Long Term Capital Management, froze financial markets in much the same way that the failure of Lehman Brothers would freeze markets a decade later. An ad hoc rescue cobbled together by Federal Reserve officials averted disaster in 1998, but the event should have served as a warning, an object lesson in the dangers of out-of-control finance. (I got some of this into the original, 1999 edition of *The Return of Depression Economics*, where I drew parallels between the LTCM crisis and the financial crises then sweeping through Asia. In retrospect, however, I failed to see just how broad the problem was.)

But the lesson was ignored. Right up to the crisis of 2008, movers and shakers insisted, as Greenspan did in the quotation that opened this chapter, that all was well. Moreover, they routinely claimed that financial deregulation had led to greatly improved overall economic performance. To this day it's common to hear assertions like this one from Eugene Fama, a famous and influential financial economist at the University of Chicago:

> Beginning in the early 1980s, the developed world and some big players in the developing world experienced a period of extraordinary growth. It's reasonable to argue that in facilitating the flow of world savings to productive uses around the world, financial markets and financial institutions played a big role in this growth.

Fama wrote this, by the way, in November 2009, in the midst of a slump most of us blamed in part on runaway finance. But even over the longer term, nothing like his vision of "extraor-

dinary growth" happened. In the United States, growth in
the decades following deregulation was actually slower than
in the preceding decades; the true period of "extraordinary
growth" was the generation that followed World War II, during which living standards more or less doubled. In fact, for
middle-income families, even before the crisis there was only
a modest rise in income under deregulation, achieved mainly
though longer working hours rather than higher wages.

For a small but influential minority, however, the era of
financial deregulation and growing debt was indeed a time of
extraordinary income growth. And that, surely, is an important reason so few were willing to listen to warnings about the
path the economy was taking.

To understand the deeper reasons for our current crisis, in
short, we need to talk about income inequality and the coming of a second Gilded Age.

CHAPTER FIVE

THE SECOND GILDED AGE

Owning and maintaining a house the size of the Taj Mahal is expensive. Kerry Delrose, director of interior design at Jones Footer Margeotes Partners in Greenwich, helpfully walked me through the cost of decorating a mansion appropriately. "Carpeting is very expensive," he said, mentioning a $74,000 broadloom carpet he had ordered for a client's bedroom. "And drapery. Just on the hardware—poles, finials, brackets, rings—you spend several thousand dollars, easily $10,000 alone per room just for hardware. Then the fabrics . . . For most of these rooms, the grand room, the family room, you need 100 to 150 yards of fabric. That's not uncommon. Cotton fabrics are $40 to $60 a yard on average, but most of the ones we look at, the really good silks, are $100 a yard."

So far, the curtains for just one room have come in at $20,000 to $25,000.

—"Greenwich's Outrageous Fortune," *Vanity Fair*, July 2006

IN 2006, JUST before the financial system started to come apart at the seams, Nina Munk wrote an article for *Vanity Fair* about the mansion-building spree then going on in Greenwich, Connecticut. As she noted, Greenwich had been a favorite haunt of tycoons in the early twentieth century, a place where the creators or inheritors of industrial fortunes built mansions "to rival the palazzi and châteaux and stately homes of Europe." Post–World War II America was, however, a place where few people could afford to keep up a twenty-five-room mansion; bit by bit, the great estates were broken up and sold off.

Then the hedge fund managers started moving in.

Much of the financial industry is, of course, concentrated in Wall Street (and in the City of London, which plays a similar role). But hedge funds—which basically speculate with borrowed money, and which attract investors who hope that their managers have the special insight it takes to make a killing—have congregated in Greenwich, which is about a forty-minute train ride from Manhattan. The managers of those funds have incomes as big as or bigger than those of the robber barons of yore, even after adjusting for inflation. In 2006 the twenty-five highest-paid hedge fund managers made $14 billion, three times the combined salaries of New York City's eighty thousand schoolteachers.

When such men decided to buy houses in Greenwich, price was no object. They cheerfully bought up the old Gilded Age mansions, and in many cases knocked them down to build even bigger palaces. How big? According to Munk, the average new home purchased by a hedge fund manager was around 15,000 square feet. One manager, Larry Feinberg of Oracle Partners, a hedge fund specializing in the health care industry, bought a $20 million home simply to knock it down; his building plans, filed with the town, called for a 30,771-square-foot villa. As Munk helpfully noted, that's only slightly smaller than the Taj Mahal.

But why should we care? Is it just prurient interest? Well, I can't deny that there is a certain fascination in reading about lifestyles of the rich and fatuous. But there's a larger point here as well.

I noted at the end of chapter 4 that even before the crisis of 2008 it was hard to see why financial deregulation was considered a success story. The savings and loan mess had provided an expensive demonstration of how deregulated bankers could run wild; there had been near-misses that foreshadowed the crisis to come; and economic growth had, if anything, been lower in the era of deregulation than it had been in the era of tight regulation. Yet there was (and still is) a strange delusion among some commentators—by and large, although not entirely, on the political right—that the era of deregulation was one of economic triumph. In the preceding chapter I observed that Eugene Fama, a celebrated finance theorist at the University of Chicago, declared that the era since financial deregulation began has been one of "extraordinary growth," when it has in fact been nothing of the sort.

What might have led Fama to believe that we'd been experiencing extraordinary growth? Well, maybe it was the fact that *some* people—the kind of people who, say, sponsor conferences on financial theory—did indeed experience extraordinary growth in their income.

I offer two figures on page 74. The figure on the top shows two measures of U.S. family income since World War II, both in inflation-adjusted dollars. One is average family income—total income divided by the number of families. Even this measure shows no hint of "extraordinary growth" following financial deregulation. In fact, growth was faster before 1980 than after. The second shows *median* family income—the income of the typical family, with income higher than that of half the population, lower than that of the other half. As you can see, the income of the typical family grew much less after 1980 than before. Why? Because so many of the fruits of economic growth went to a handful of people at the top.

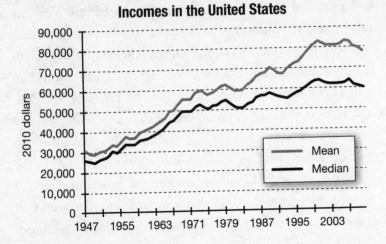

Even mean income—the income of the average family—didn't take off in the age of deregulation, while the growth of median income—the income of families in the middle of the income distribution—slowed to a crawl . . .

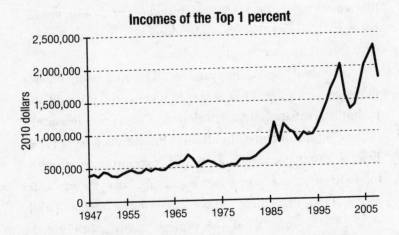

. . . but average incomes for the top 1 percent of the population exploded.

Source: U.S. Census, Thomas Piketty and Emmanuel Saez, "Income Inequality in the United States: 1913–1998," *Quarterly Journal of Economics*, February 2003 (2010 revision)

The figure on the bottom shows just how well people at the top—in this case, the "1 percent" made famous by Occupy Wall

Street—actually did. For them growth since financial deregulation has indeed been extraordinary; their incomes adjusted for inflation fluctuated with the rise and fall of the stock market, but more or less quadrupled since 1980. So the elite did very, very well under deregulation, while the super-elite and the super-duper-elite—the top 0.1 percent and the top 0.01 percent—did even better, with the richest one–ten thousandth of Americans seeing a 660 percent gain. And that's what lies behind the proliferation of Taj Mahals in Connecticut.

The remarkable rise of the very rich, even in the face of lackluster economic growth and very modest gains for the middle class, poses two main questions. One is why it happened—a subject I'll address only briefly, since it isn't the main theme of this book. The other is what it has to do with the depression we find ourselves experiencing, which is a tricky but important subject.

First, then, what's with those surging incomes at the top?

Why Did the Rich Get (So Much) Richer?

To this day, many discussions of rising inequality make it sound as if it's all about a growing premium for skill. Modern technology, the story goes, creates a rising demand for highly educated workers while diminishing the need for routine and/or physical labor. So the well-educated minority pulls ahead of the less-educated majority. For example, back in 2006 Ben Bernanke, the chairman of the Fed, gave a speech on rising inequality in which he suggested that the main story is one in which the highly educated top 20 percent of workers were pulling away from the less-educated bottom 80 percent.

And to be honest, this story isn't completely wrong: in general, the more education you have, the better you and people like you have done these past thirty years. Wages of college-educated Americans have risen compared with those of Americans with no more than a high school education, and wages of Americans with a postgraduate degree have risen compared with those of Americans with only a bachelor's.

To focus solely on education-based wage differentials, however, is to miss not just part of the story but most of it. For the really big gains have gone not to college-educated workers in general but to a handful of the very well-off. High school teachers generally have both college and postgraduate degrees; they have not, to put it mildly, seen the kinds of income gains that hedge fund managers have experienced. Remember, again, how twenty-five fund managers made three times as much money as the eighty thousand New York City schoolteachers.

The Occupy Wall Street movement rallied around a slogan, "We are the 99 percent," which got much closer to the truth than the usual establishment talk about education and skill differentials. And it's not just radicals who are saying this. Last fall the painstakingly nonpartisan, ultra-respectable Congressional Budget Office (CBO) put out a report detailing the rise in inequality between 1979 and 2007; it found that Americans in the 80th to 99th percentiles—that is, Bernanke's top 20 percent, minus OWS's 1 percent—had seen an income rise of 65 percent over that period. That's pretty good, especially compared with families lower down the scale: families near the middle did only about half that well, and the bottom 20 percent saw only an 18 percent gain. But the top 1 percent saw its income rise 277.5 percent, and, as we've already seen, the top 0.1 percent and the top 0.01 percent saw even bigger gains.

And the rising incomes of the very affluent were by no means a sideshow when we ask where the gains from economic growth went. According to the CBO, the share of after-tax income going to the top 1 percent rose from 7.7 percent to 17.1 percent of total income; that is, other things equal, a roughly 10 percent reduction in the amount of income left over for everyone else. Alternatively, we can ask how much of the overall rise in inequality was due to the way the 1 percent pulled away from everyone else; according to a widely used measure of inequality (the Gini index), the answer is that the shift of income to the top 1 percent was responsible for about half the rise.

So why did the top 1 percent, and even better the top 0.1 percent, do so much better than everyone else?

That is by no means a settled issue among economists, and the reasons for this uncertainty are themselves revealing. First of all, until quite recently there was a sense among many economists that the incomes of the very rich weren't a proper subject for study, that the issue belonged in tabloids obsessed with celebrities rather than in the pages of sober economics journals. It wasn't until quite late in the game that the realization sank in that the incomes of the rich, far from being a trivial issue, are at the heart of what has been happening to America's economy and society.

And even once economists began taking the 1 percent and the 0.1 percent seriously, they found the subject unwelcoming in two senses. Merely to raise the issue was to enter a political war zone: income distribution at the top is one of those areas where anyone who raises his head above the parapet will encounter fierce attacks from what amount to hired guns protecting the interests of the wealthy. For example, a few years ago Thomas Piketty and Emmanuel Saez, whose work has been crucial in tracking the long-run ups and downs of inequality, found themselves under fire from Alan Reynolds of the Cato Institute, who has spent decades asserting that inequality hasn't really increased; every time one of his arguments is thoroughly debunked, he pops up with another.

Furthermore, politics aside, incomes at the very top are not a congenial subject for the tools economists usually rely on. What my profession mostly knows is supply and demand—yes, there's much more to economics, but that's the first and primary tool of analysis. And recipients of high incomes don't live in a supply-and-demand world.

Recent work by the economists Jon Bakija, Adam Cole, and Bradley Heim gives us a good sense of who the top 0.1 percent are. The short answer is that they're basically corporate executives or financial wheeler-dealers. Almost half the income of the top 0.1 goes to executives and managers in non-financial firms; another fifth goes to people in finance; throw in lawyers and people in real estate, and you're up to about three-quarters of the total.

Now, textbook economics says that in a competitive market, each worker gets paid his or her "marginal product"—the amount that the worker adds to total production. But what's the marginal product of a corporate executive, or a hedge fund manager, or for that matter of a corporate lawyer? Nobody really knows. And if you look at how incomes for people in this class are actually determined, you find processes that arguably bear very little relationship to their economic contribution.

At this point someone is likely to say, "But what about Steve Jobs or Mark Zuckerberg? Didn't they get rich by creating products of value?" And the answer is yes—but very few of the top 1 percent, or even the top 0.01 percent, made their money that way. For the most part, we're looking at executives at firms that they didn't themselves create. They may own a lot of stock or stock options in their companies, but they received those assets as part of their pay package, not by founding the business. And who decides what goes into their pay packages? Well, CEOs famously have their pay set by compensation committees appointed by . . . the same CEOs they're judging.

Top earners in the financial industry operate in a more competitive environment, but there are good reasons to believe that their earnings are often inflated compared with their actual achievements. Hedge fund managers, for example, get paid both fees for the job of managing other people's money and a percentage of their profits. This gives them every incentive to make risky, highly leveraged investments: if things go well, they are richly rewarded, whereas if and when things go badly, they don't have to return their previous gains. The result is that on average—that is, once you take into account the fact that many hedge funds fail, and investors don't know in advance which funds will end up part of the casualty list—investors in hedge funds don't do particularly well. In fact, according to one recent book, *The Hedge Fund Mirage*, by Simon Lack, over the past decade investors in hedge funds would, on average, have done better putting their money in Treasury bills—and may have made no money at all.

You might think that investors would become wise to these skewed incentives, and more broadly that they would come to appreciate what every prospectus says: "past performance is no guarantee of future results," that is, a manager who did well by investors last year may just have been lucky. But the evidence suggests that many investors—and not just unsophisticated little guys—remain gullible, placing their faith in the genius of financial players despite abundant evidence that this is normally a losing proposition.

One more thing: even when the financial wheeler-dealers

made money for investors, in important cases they did so not by creating value for society as a whole but by in effect expropriating value from other players.

This is most obvious in the case of bad banking. In the 1980s owners of savings and loans made big profits by taking big risks—then left taxpayers holding the bag. In the 2000s bankers did it again, amassing vast fortunes by making bad real estate loans and either selling them to unwitting investors or receiving a government bailout when crisis struck.

But it's also true of a lot of private equity, the business of buying companies, restructuring them, then selling them off again. (Gordon Gekko, in the movie *Wall Street*, was a private-equity player; Mitt Romney was one in real life.) To be fair, some private-equity firms have done valuable work by financing start-ups, in high-tech and elsewhere. In many other cases, however, profits have come from what Larry Summers—yes, that Larry Summers—called, in an influential paper of the same name, "breach of trust": basically, breaking contracts and agreements. Consider, for example, the case of Simmons Bedding, a storied company founded in 1870 that declared bankruptcy in 2009, causing many workers to lose their jobs and lenders to lose much of their stake as well. Here's how the *New York Times* described the run-up to bankruptcy:

> For many of the company's investors, the sale will be a disaster. Its bondholders alone stand to lose more than $575 million. The company's downfall has also devastated employees like Noble Rogers, who worked for 22 years at Simmons, most of that time at a factory outside Atlanta. He is one of 1,000 employees—more than one-quarter of the work force—laid off last year.

But Thomas H. Lee Partners of Boston has not only escaped unscathed, it has made a profit. The investment firm, which bought Simmons in 2003, has pocketed around $77 million in profit, even as the company's fortunes have declined. THL collected hundreds of millions of dollars from the company in the form of special dividends. It also paid itself millions more in fees, first for buying the company, then for helping run it.

Incomes at the top, then, aren't much like incomes farther down the scale; they are much less obviously related either to economic fundamentals or to contributions to the economy as a whole. But why should those incomes have skyrocketed beginning around 1980?

Part of the explanation surely rests with the financial deregulation I discussed in chapter 4. The tightly regulated financial markets that characterized America between the 1930s and the 1970s didn't offer the opportunities for self-enrichment that flourished after 1980. And high incomes in finance arguably had a "contagion" effect on executive pay more broadly. If nothing else, enormous paychecks on Wall Street surely made it easier for compensation committees to claim justification for big salaries in the nonfinance world.

Thomas Piketty and Emmanuel Saez, whose work I've already mentioned, have argued that top incomes are strongly affected by social norms. Their view is echoed by researchers like Lucian Bebchuck of the Harvard Law School, who argues that the main limitation on CEO pay is the "outrage constraint." Such arguments suggest that changes in the political climate after 1980 may have cleared the way for what amounts to the raw exercise of power to claim high incomes, in a way that wasn't considered doable earlier. It's surely relevant here to note the sharp decline in unionization during the 1980s, which removed one major player that might have protested huge paychecks for executives.

Recently Piketty and Saez have added a further argument: sharp cuts in taxes on high incomes, they suggest, have actually encouraged executives to push the envelope further, to engage in "rent-seeking" at the expense of the rest of the workforce. Why? Because the personal payoff to a higher pretax income has risen, making executives more willing to risk condemnation and/or hurt morale by pursuing personal gain. As Piketty and Saez note, there is a fairly close negative correlation between top tax rates and the top 1 percent's share of income, both over time and across countries.

What I take from all this is that we should probably think of rapidly rising incomes at the top as reflecting the same social and political factors that promoted lax financial regulation. Lax regulation, as we've already seen, is crucial to understanding how we got into this crisis. But did inequality per se also play an important role?

Inequality and Crises

Before the financial crisis of 2008 struck, I would often give talks to lay audiences about income inequality, in which I would point out that top income shares had risen to levels not seen since 1929. Invariably there would be questions about whether that meant that we were on the verge of another Great Depression—and I would declare that this wasn't necessarily so, that there was no reason extreme inequality would necessarily cause economic disaster.

Well, whaddya know?

Still, correlation is not the same as causation. The fact that a return to pre-Depression levels of inequality was followed by a return to depression economics could be just a coincidence. Or it could reflect common causes of both phenomena. What do we really know here, and what might we suspect?

Common causation is almost surely part of the story. There was a major political turn to the right in the United States, the United Kingdom, and to some extent other countries circa 1980. This rightward turn led both to policy changes, especially large reductions in top tax rates, and to a change in social norms—a relaxation of the "outrage constraint"—that played a significant role in the sudden surge of top incomes. And the same rightward turn led to financial deregulation and the failure to regulate new forms of banking, which as we saw in chapter 4 did a lot to set the stage for crisis.

But is there also an arrow of causation running directly from income inequality to financial crisis? Maybe, but it's a harder case to make.

For example, one popular story about inequality and crisis—that the rising share of income going to the rich has undermined overall demand, because of the shrinking purchasing power of the middle class—just doesn't work when you look at the data. "Underconsumption" stories depend on the notion that as income becomes concentrated in the hands of a few, consumer spending lags, and savings rise faster than investment opportunities. In reality, however, consumer spending in the United States remained strong despite growing inequality, and far from rising, personal saving was on a long downward trend during the era of financial deregulation and rising inequality.

A better case can be made for the opposite proposition—

that rising inequality has led to too much consumption rather than too little and, more specifically, that the widening gaps in income have caused those left behind to take on too much debt. Robert Frank of Cornell has argued that rising incomes at the top lead to "expenditure cascades" that end up reducing savings and increasing debt:

> The rich have been spending more simply because they have so much extra money. Their spending shifts the frame of reference that shapes the demands of those just below them, who travel in overlapping social circles. So this second group, too, spends more, which shifts the frame of reference for the group just below it, and so on, all the way down the income ladder. These cascades have made it substantially more expensive for middle-class families to achieve basic financial goals.

A similar message comes out of work by Elizabeth Warren and Amelia Tyagi, whose 2004 book *The Two-Income Trap* traces the rising tide of personal bankruptcies, which began well before the overall financial crisis, and should have been seen as a warning sign. (Warren, a professor at Harvard Law School, has become a leading crusader for financial reform: the new Consumer Financial Protection Bureau is her creation. And she is now running for the Senate.) They showed that a big factor in these bankruptcies was the growing inequality of public education, which in turn reflected rising income inequality: middle-class families stretched to buy homes in good school districts, and in the process they took on levels of debt that made them highly vulnerable to job loss or illness.

This is a serious and important argument. But my guess— and it can't be more than that, given how little we understand

some of these channels of influence—is that the biggest contribution of rising inequality to the depression we're in was and
is political. When we ask why policy makers were so blind to
the risks of financial deregulation—and, since 2008, why they
have been so blind to the risks of an inadequate response to
the economic slump—it's hard not to recall Upton Sinclair's
famous line: "It is difficult to get a man to understand something, when his salary depends on his not understanding it."
Money buys influence; big money buys big influence; and the
policies that got us where we are, while they never did much
for most people, were, for a while at least, very good to a few
people at the top.

The Elite and the Political Economy of Bad Policies

In 1998, as I mentioned in chapter 4, Citicorp—the holding
company for Citibank—merged with Travelers Group to form
what we now know as Citigroup. The deal was a crowning
achievement for Sandy Weill, who became the CEO of the
new financial giant. But there was a small problem: the merger
was illegal. Travelers was an insurance company that had also
acquired two investment banks, Smith Barney and Shearson
Lehman. And under Glass-Steagall, commercial banks like
Citi couldn't engage in either insurance or investment banking.

So, modern America being the kind of place it is, Weill
set out to get the law changed, with the help of Senator Phil
Gramm of Texas, the chairman of the Senate Committee on
Banking, Housing, and Urban Affairs. In that role, he championed a number of deregulatory measures; the crown jewel,
however, was the Gramm-Leach-Bliley Act of 1999, which
effectively repealed Glass-Steagall, and retroactively legalized
the Citi-Travelers merger.

Why was Gramm so accommodating? No doubt he sincerely believed in the virtues of deregulation. But he also had substantial inducements to reinforce his belief. While he was still in office, he received large campaign contributions from the financial industry, which was his biggest supporter. And when he left office, he joined the board of directors of UBS, another financial giant. But let's not make this a partisan thing. Democrats also supported the repeal of Glass-Steagall and of financial deregulation in general. The key figure in the decision to support Gramm's initiative was Robert Rubin, who was Treasury secretary at the time. Before entering government, Rubin was co-chairman of Goldman Sachs; after leaving government, he became vice chairman of . . . Citigroup.

I've met Rubin a number of times, and doubt that he's a bought man—if nothing else, he was already so rich that he didn't really need that postgovernment job. Still, he took it. And as for Gramm, to the best of my knowledge he sincerely believed and believes in all the positions he has taken. Nonetheless, the fact that taking those positions filled his campaign coffers when he was in the Senate, and topped up his personal bank account thereafter, must have made his policy beliefs, shall we say, easier to hold.

In general, we should think of the role of money in shaping politics as being something that takes place on many levels. There's plenty of raw corruption—politicians who are simply bought, either with campaign contributions or with personal payoffs. But in many, perhaps most cases, the corruption is softer and less identifiable: politicians are rewarded for holding certain positions, and this makes them hold those positions more firmly, until in their own mind they're not really being bought, yet from the outside it's hard to tell the difference between what they "really" believe and what they're paid to believe.

At a still more amorphous level, wealth brings access, and access brings personal influence. Top bankers can get into the White House or senators' offices in a way that the man on the street can't. Once in those offices, they can be persuasive, not just because of the gifts they offer but because of who they are. The rich are different from you and me, and not just because they have better tailors: they have the confidence, the air of knowing what to do, that comes with worldly success. Their lifestyles are seductive even if you have no intention of doing what it takes to afford a similar style yourself. And in the case of Wall Street types, at least, they really do tend to be very smart people and hence impressive in conversation.

The kind of influence the rich can have even on an honest politician was nicely summarized long ago by H. L. Mencken, describing the decline of Al Smith, who went from crusading reformer to bitter opponent of the New Deal: "The Al of today is no longer a politician of the first chop. His association with the rich has apparently wobbled and changed him. He has become a golf player . . ."

Now, all of this has been true throughout history. But the gravitational political pull of the rich becomes stronger when the rich are richer. Consider, for example, the revolving door, in which politicians and officials end up going to work for the industry they were supposed to oversee. That door has existed for a long time, but the salary you can get if the industry likes you is vastly higher than it used to be, which has to make the urge to accommodate the people on the other side of that door, to adopt positions that will make you an attractive hire in your postpolicy career, much stronger than it was thirty years ago.

This pull doesn't just apply to policy and events within the United States. *Slate*'s Matthew Yglesias, meditating on the surprising willingness of political leaders in Europe to go along with harsh austerity measures, offered a speculation based on personal interests:

> Normally you would think that a national prime minister's best option is to try to do the stuff that's likely to get him re-elected. No matter how bleak the outlook, this is your dominant strategy. But in the era of globalization and EU-ification, I think the leaders of small countries are actually in a somewhat different situation. If you leave office held in high esteem by the Davos set, there are any number of European Commission or IMF or whatnot gigs that you might be eligible for even if you're absolutely despised by your fellow countrymen. Indeed, in some ways being absolutely despised would be a plus. The ultimate demonstration of solidarity to the "international community" would be to do what the international community wants even in the face of massive resistance from your domestic political constituency.
>
> My guess is that even if Brian Cowen turns out to have permanently destroyed the once-dominant Fianna Fail, he has a promising future on the international circuit talking about the need for "tough choices."

One more thing: while the influence of the financial industry has been strong on both parties in the United States, the broader impact of big money on politics has tended to be stronger on Republicans, who are ideologically more inclined to support the interests of the top 1 percent or the top 0.1 percent in any case. This differential interest probably explains a striking finding by the political scientists Keith Poole and Howard Rosenthal, who used the results of congressional votes to measure political polarization, the gap between the parties, over roughly the past century. They discovered a strong correlation between the share of the top 1 percent in total income and the degree of polarization in Congress. The first thirty years after World War II, which were marked by a relatively equal distribution of income, were also marked by a lot of actual bipartisanship, with a substantial group of centrist politicians making decisions more or less by consensus. Since 1980, however, the Republican Party has moved right in tandem with the rising incomes of the elite, and political compromise has become almost impossible.

Which brings me back to the relationship between inequality and the new depression.

The growing influence of the wealthy led to many policy choices that liberals like me don't like—the reduced progressivity of taxes, the shortchanging of aid to the poor, the decline of public education, and so on. Most relevant for the subject of this book, however, was the way the political system persisted with deregulation and nonregulation despite many warning signs that an unregulated financial system was a recipe for trouble.

The point is that this persistence seems a lot less puzzling once you take into account the growing influence of the very rich. For one thing, quite a few of those very rich were making their money from unregulated finance, so they had a direct stake in the continuation of the movements against regulation. Beyond that, whatever questions might have been raised about overall economic performance after 1980, the economy was working extremely well, thank you, for the people at the top.

So while rising inequality probably wasn't the main direct

cause of the crisis, it created a political environment in which
it was impossible to notice or act on the warning signs. As
we'll see in the next two chapters, it also created both an intellectual and a political environment that crippled our ability to
respond effectively when crisis struck.

CHAPTER SIX

DARK AGE ECONOMICS

Macroeconomics was born as a distinct field in the 1940s, as a part of the intellectual response to the Great Depression. The term then referred to the body of knowledge and expertise that we hoped would prevent the recurrence of that economic disaster. My thesis in this lecture is that macroeconomics in this original sense has succeeded: Its central problem of depression-prevention has been solved, for all practical purposes, and has in fact been solved for many decades.

—Robert Lucas, presidential address to the
American Economic Association, 2003

GIVEN WHAT WE know now, Robert Lucas's confident assertion that depressions were a thing of the past sounds very much like famous last words. Actually, to some of us they sounded like famous last words even at the time: the Asian financial crisis of 1997–98 and the persistent troubles of Japan bore a clear resemblance to what happened in the 1930s, raising real questions about whether things were anywhere near being under control. I wrote a book about those doubts, *The Return of Depression Economics*, originally published in 1999; I released a revised edition in 2008, when all of my nightmares came true.

Yet Lucas, a Nobel laureate who was a towering, almost

dominant figure in macroeconomics for much of the 1970s and 1980s, wasn't wrong to say that economists had learned a lot since the 1930s. By, say, 1970 the economics profession really did know enough to prevent a recurrence of anything resembling the Great Depression.

And then much of the profession proceeded to forget what it had learned.

As we try to cope with the depression we're in, it has been distressing to see the extent to which economists have been part of the problem, not part of the solution. Many, though not all, leading economists argued in favor of financial deregulation even as it made the economy ever more vulnerable to crisis. Then, when crisis struck, all too many famous economists argued, fiercely and ignorantly, against any kind of effective response. And, sad to say, one of those making arguments that were both ignorant and destructive was none other than Robert Lucas.

Some three years ago, when I realized how the profession was failing in its moment of truth, I coined a phrase for what I was seeing: a "dark age of macroeconomics." My point was that this was different from what had happened in the 1930s, when nobody knew how to think about a depression and it took pathbreaking economic thinking to find a way forward. That era was, if you like, the Stone Age of economics, when the arts of civilization had yet to be discovered. But by 2009 the arts of civilization had been discovered—and then lost. A new barbarism had descended on the field.

How could that have happened? It involved, I think, a mixture of politics and runaway academic sociology.

Keynesophobia

In 2008 we suddenly found ourselves living in a Keynesian world—that is, a world that very much had the features John Maynard Keynes focused on in his 1936 magnum opus, *The General Theory of Employment, Interest, and Money.* By that I mean that we found ourselves in a world in which lack of sufficient demand had become the key economic problem, and in which narrow technocratic solutions, like cuts in the Federal Reserve's interest rate target, were not adequate to that situation. To deal effectively with the crisis, we needed more activist government policies, in the form both of temporary spending to support employment and of efforts to reduce the overhang of mortgage debt.

One might think that these solutions could still be considered technocratic, and separated from the broader question of income distribution. Keynes himself described his theory as "moderately conservative in its implications," consistent with an economy run on the principles of private enterprise. From the beginning, however, political conservatives—especially those most concerned with defending the position of the wealthy—fiercely opposed Keynesian ideas.

And I mean fiercely. Paul Samuelson's textbook *Economics*, whose first edition was published in 1948, is widely credited with bringing Keynesian economics to American colleges. But it was actually the second entry. A previous book, by the Canadian economist Lorie Tarshis, was effectively blackballed by right-wing opposition, including an organized campaign that successfully induced many universities to drop the book. Later, in his *God and Man at Yale*, William F. Buckley would direct much of his ire at Yale for allowing the teaching of Keynesian economics.

The tradition has continued through the years. In 2005 the right-wing magazine *Human Events* listed Keynes's *General Theory* among the ten most harmful books of the nineteenth and twentieth centuries, right up there with *Mein Kampf* and *Das Kapital*.

Why such animus against a book with a "moderately conservative" message? Part of the answer seems to be that even though the government intervention called for by Keynesian economics is modest and targeted, conservatives have always seen it as the thin edge of the wedge: concede that the government can play a useful role in fighting slumps, and the next thing you know we'll be living under socialism. The rhetorical amalgamation of Keynesianism with central planning and radical redistribution—although explicitly denied by Keynes himself, who declared, "There are valuable human activities which require the motive of money-making and the environment of private wealth-ownership for their full fruition"—is almost universal on the right, including among economists who really should know better.

There is also the motive suggested by Keynes's contemporary Michal Kalecki (who, for the record, actually was a socialist) in a classic 1943 essay:

We shall deal first with the reluctance of the "captains of industry" to accept government intervention in the matter of employment. Every widening of state activity is looked upon by business with suspicion, but the creation of employment by government spending has a special aspect which makes the opposition particularly intense. Under a laissez-faire system the level of employment depends to a great extent on the so-called state of confidence. If this deteriorates, private investment declines, which results in a fall of output and employment (both directly and through the secondary effect of the fall in incomes upon consumption and investment). This gives the capitalists a powerful indirect control over government policy: everything which may shake the state of confidence must be carefully avoided because it would cause an economic crisis. But once the government learns the trick of increasing employment by its own purchases, this powerful controlling device loses its effectiveness. Hence budget deficits necessary to carry out government intervention must be regarded as perilous. The social function of the doctrine of "sound finance" is to make the level of employment dependent on the state of confidence.

This sounded a bit extreme to me the first time I read it, but it now seems all too plausible. These days you can see the "confidence" argument being deployed all the time. For example, here is how the real estate and media mogul Mort Zuckerman began an op-ed in the *Financial Times* aimed at dissuading President Obama from taking any kind of populist line:

The growing tension between the Obama administration and business is a cause for national concern. The president has lost the confidence of employers, whose worries over taxes and the increased costs of new regulation are holding back investment and growth. The government must appreciate that confidence is an imperative if business is to invest, take risks and put the millions of unemployed back to productive work.

There was and is, in fact, no evidence that "worries over taxes and the increased costs of new regulation" are playing any significant role in holding the economy back. Kalecki's point,

however, was that arguments like this would fall completely
flat if there was widespread public acceptance of the notion
that Keynesian policies could create jobs. So there is a special
animus against direct government job-creation policies, above
and beyond the generalized fear that Keynesian ideas might
legitimize government intervention in general.

Put these motives together, and you can see why writers
and institutions with close ties to the upper tail of the income
distribution have been consistently hostile to Keynesian ideas.
That has not changed over the seventy-five years since Keynes
wrote the *General Theory*. What has changed, however, is the
wealth and hence influence of that upper tail. These days conservatives have moved far to the right even of Milton Friedman, who at least conceded that monetary policy could be an
effective tool for stabilizing the economy. Views that were on
the political fringe forty years ago are now part of the received
doctrine of one of our two major political parties.

A touchier subject is the extent to which the vested interest
of the 1 percent, or better yet the 0.1 percent, has colored the
discussion among academic economists. But surely that influence must have been there: if nothing else, the preferences of
university donors, the availability of fellowships and lucrative
consulting contracts, and so on must have encouraged the profession not just to turn away from Keynesian ideas but to forget
much that had been learned in the 1930s and 1940s.

Yet this influence of wealth wouldn't have gone so far if it
hadn't been assisted by a kind of runaway academic sociology,
through which basically absurd notions became dogma in the
analysis of both finance and macroeconomics.

Notably Rare Exceptions

In the 1930s, financial markets, for obvious reasons, didn't get much respect. Keynes compared them to

> those newspaper competitions in which the competitors have to pick out the six prettiest faces from a hundred photographs, the prize being awarded to the competitor whose choice most nearly corresponds to the average preferences of the competitors as a whole; so that each competitor has to pick, not those faces which he himself finds prettiest, but those that he thinks likeliest to catch the fancy of the other competitors.

And Keynes considered it a very bad idea to let such markets, in which speculators spent their time chasing one another's tails, dictate important business decisions: "When the capital development of a country becomes a by-product of the activities of a casino, the job is likely to be ill-done."

By 1970 or so, however, the study of financial markets seemed to have been taken over by Voltaire's Dr. Pangloss, who insisted that we live in the best of all possible worlds. Discussion of investor irrationality, of bubbles, of destructive speculation had virtually disappeared from academic discourse. The field was dominated by the "efficient-markets hypothesis," promulgated by Eugene Fama of the University of Chicago, which claims that financial markets price assets precisely at their intrinsic worth, given all publicly available information. (The price of a company's stock, for example, always accurately reflects the company's value, given the information available on the company's earnings, its business prospects,

and so on.) And by the 1980s, finance economists, notably
Michael Jensen of the Harvard Business School, were arguing
that because financial markets always get prices right, the best
thing corporate chieftains can do, not just for themselves but
for the sake of the economy, is to maximize their stock prices.
In other words, finance economists believed that we *should*
put the capital development of the nation in the hands of what
Keynes called a "casino."

It's hard to argue that this transformation in the profession
was driven by events. True, the memory of 1929 was gradually
receding, but there continued to be bull markets, with widespread tales of speculative excess, followed by bear markets.
In 1973–74, for example, stocks lost 48 percent of their value.
And the 1987 stock crash, in which the Dow plunged nearly
23 percent in a day for no clear reason, should have raised at
least a few doubts about market rationality.

These events, however, which Keynes would have considered evidence of the unreliability of markets, did little to
blunt the force of a beautiful idea. The theoretical model that
finance economists developed by assuming that every investor
rationally balances risk against reward—the so-called Capital Asset Pricing Model, or CAPM (pronounced cap-em)—is
wonderfully elegant. And if you accept its premises, it's also
extremely useful. CAPM not only tells you how to choose
your portfolio; even more important from the financial industry's point of view, it also tells you how to put a price on financial derivatives, claims on claims. The elegance and apparent
usefulness of the new theory led to a string of Nobel Prizes for
its creators, and many of the theory's adepts also received more
mundane rewards: armed with their new models and formi-
dable math skills—the more arcane uses of CAPM require

physicist-level computations—mild-mannered business school professors could and did become Wall Street rocket scientists, earning Wall Street paychecks.

To be fair, finance theorists didn't accept the efficient-markets hypothesis merely because it was elegant, convenient, and lucrative. They also produced a great deal of statistical evidence, which at first seemed strongly supportive. But this evidence was of an oddly limited form. Finance economists rarely asked the seemingly obvious (though not easily answered) question of whether asset prices made sense given real-world fundamentals like earnings. Instead, they asked only whether asset prices made sense given other asset prices. Larry Summers, who was President Obama's top economic adviser for much of his first three years, once mocked finance professors with a parable about "ketchup economists" who "have shown that two-quart bottles of ketchup invariably sell for exactly twice as much as one-quart bottles of ketchup," and conclude from this that the ketchup market is perfectly efficient.

But neither this mockery nor more polite critiques from other economists had much effect. Finance theorists continued to believe that their models were essentially right, and so did many people making real-world decisions. Not least among these was Alan Greenspan, whose rejection of calls to rein in subprime lending or address the ever-inflating housing bubble rested in large part on the belief that modern financial economics had everything under control.

Now, you might imagine that the scale of the financial disaster that struck the world in 2008, and the way in which all those supposedly sophisticated financial tools turned into instruments of disaster, must have shaken the grip of efficient-markets theory. But you would be wrong.

True, just after Lehman Brothers fell, Greenspan declared himself in a state of "shocked disbelief," because "the whole intellectual edifice" had "collapsed." By March 2011, however, he was back to his old position, calling for a repeal of the (very modest) attempts to tighten financial regulation in the wake of the crisis. Financial markets were fine, he wrote in the *Financial Times*: "With notably rare exceptions (2008, for example), the global 'invisible hand' has created relatively stable exchange rates, interest rates, prices, and wage rates."

Hey, what's an occasional world-economy-destroying crisis? The political scientist Henry Farrell, in a blog post, quickly responded by inviting readers to find other uses for the "notably rare exceptions" construction—for example, "With notably rare exceptions, Japanese nuclear reactors have been safe from earthquakes."

And the sad thing is that Greenspan's response has been widely shared. There has been remarkably little rethinking on the part of finance theorists. Eugene Fama, the father of the efficient-markets hypothesis, has given no ground at all; the crisis, he asserts, was caused by government intervention, especially the role of Fannie and Freddie (which is the Big Lie I talked about in chapter 4).

This reaction is understandable, though not forgivable. For either Greenspan or Fama to admit how far off the rails finance theory went would be to admit that they had spent much of their careers pursuing a blind alley. The same can be said of some leading macroeconomists, who similarly spent decades pushing a view of how the economy works that has been utterly refuted by recent events, and have similarly been unwilling to admit their misjudgment.

But that's not all: in defending their mistakes, they have also played a significant role in undermining an effective response to the depression we're in.

Whispers and Giggles

In 1965 *Time* magazine quoted none other than Milton Friedman as declaring that "we are all Keynesians now." Friedman tried to walk the quotation back a bit, but it was true: although Friedman was the champion of a doctrine known as monetarism that was sold as an alternative to Keynes, it wasn't really all that different in its conceptual foundations. Indeed, when Friedman published a paper in 1970 titled "A Theoretical Framework for Monetary Analysis," many economists were shocked by just how similar it looked to textbook Keynesian theory. The truth is that in the 1960s macroeconomists shared a common view about what recessions were, and while they differed on the appropriate policies, these reflected practical disagreements, not a deep philosophical divide.

Since then, however, macroeconomics has divided into two great factions: "saltwater" economists (mainly in coastal U.S. universities), who have a more or less Keynesian vision of what recessions are all about; and "freshwater" economists (mainly at inland schools), who consider that vision nonsense.

Freshwater economists are, essentially, laissez-faire purists. They believe that all worthwhile economic analysis starts from the premises that people are rational and that markets work, premises that exclude by assumption the possibility of an economy laid low by a simple lack of sufficient demand.

But don't recessions look like periods in which there just isn't enough demand to employ everyone willing to work? Appearances can be deceiving, say the freshwater theorists.

Sound economics, in their view, says that overall failures of demand can't happen—and that means that they don't.

Yet recessions do happen. Why? In the 1970s the leading freshwater macroeconomist, the Nobel laureate Robert Lucas, argued that recessions were caused by temporary confusion: workers and companies had trouble distinguishing overall changes in the level of prices because of inflation from changes in their own particular business situation. And Lucas warned that any attempt to fight the business cycle would be counterproductive: activist policies, he held, would just add to the confusion.

I was a graduate student at the time this work was being done, and I remember how exciting it seemed—and how attractive its mathematical rigor, in particular, was to many young economists. Yet the "Lucas project," as it was widely called, went quickly off the rails.

What went wrong? The economists trying to provide macroeconomics with microfoundations soon got carried away, bringing to their project a sort of messianic zeal that would not take no for an answer. In particular, they triumphantly announced the death of Keynesian economics without having actually managed to provide a workable alternative. Robert Lucas, famously, declared in 1980—approvingly!—that participants in seminars would start to "whisper and giggle" whenever anyone presented Keynesian ideas. Keynes, and anyone who invoked Keynes, was banned from many classrooms and professional journals.

Yet even as the anti-Keynesians were declaring victory, their own project was failing. Their new models could not, it turned out, explain the basic facts of recessions. Yet they had in effect burned their bridges; after all the whispering and giggling, they couldn't turn around and admit the plain fact that Keynesian economics was actually looking pretty reasonable, after all.

So they plunged in deeper, moving further and further away from any realistic approach to recessions and how they happen. Much of the academic side of macroeconomics is now dominated by "real business cycle" theory, which says that recessions are the rational, indeed efficient, response to adverse technological shocks, which are themselves left unexplained—and that the reduction in employment that takes place during a recession is a voluntary decision by workers to take time off until conditions improve. If this sounds absurd, that's because it is. But it's a theory that lends itself to fancy mathematical modeling, which made real business cycle papers a good route to promotion and tenure. And the real business cycle theorists eventually had enough clout that to this day it's very difficult for young economists propounding a different view to get jobs at many major universities. (I told you that we're suffering from runaway academic sociology.)

Now, the freshwater economists didn't manage to have it all their way. Some economists responded to the evident failure of the Lucas project by giving Keynesian ideas a second look and a makeover. "New Keynesian" theory found a home in schools like MIT, Harvard, and Princeton—yes, near salt water—and also in policy-making institutions like the Fed and the International Monetary Fund. The New Keynesians were willing to deviate from the assumption of perfect markets or perfect rationality, or both, adding enough imperfections to accommodate a more or less Keynesian view of recessions. And in the saltwater view, active policy to fight recessions remained desirable.

That said, saltwater economists weren't immune to the seductive lure of rational individuals and perfect markets. They tried to keep their deviations from classical orthodoxy as limited as possible. This meant that there was no room in the prevailing models for such things as bubbles and banking-system collapse, despite the fact that such things continued to happen in the real world. Still, economic crisis didn't undermine the New Keynesians' fundamental worldview; even though they hadn't thought much about crises for the past few decades, their models didn't preclude the possibility of crises. As a result, such New Keynesians as Christy Romer or, for that matter, Ben Bernanke were able to offer useful responses to the crisis, notably big increases in lending by the Fed and temporary spending hikes by the federal government. Unfortunately, the same can't be said of the freshwater types.

By the way, in case you're wondering, I see myself as a sorta-kinda New Keynesian; I've even published papers that are very much in the New Keynesian style. I don't really buy the assumptions about rationality and markets that are embedded in many modern theoretical models, my own included, and I often turn to Old Keynesian ideas, but I see the usefulness of such models as a way to think through some issues carefully—an attitude that is actually widely shared on the saltwater side of the great divide. At a truly basic level, saltwater–freshwater is about pragmatism versus quasi-religious certainty that has only grown stronger as the evidence has challenged the One True Faith.

And the result was that instead of being helpful when crisis struck, all too many economists waged religious war instead.

Schlock Economics

For a long time it didn't seem to matter very much what was and, even more important, what wasn't being taught in graduate economics departments. Why? Because the Fed and its sister institutions had matters well in hand.

As I explained in chapter 2, fighting a garden-variety recession is fairly easy: the Fed just has to print more money, driving down interest rates. In practice the task isn't quite as simple as you might imagine, because the Fed has to gauge how much monetary medicine to give and when to stop, all in an environment where the data keep shifting and there are substantial lags before the results of any given policy are observed. But those difficulties didn't stop the Fed from trying to do its job; even as many academic macroeconomists wandered off into never-never land, the Fed kept its feet on the ground and continued to sponsor research that was relevant to its mission.

But what if the economy encountered a really severe recession, one that couldn't be contained with monetary policy? Well, that wasn't supposed to happen; in fact, Milton Friedman said it couldn't happen.

Even those who dislike many of the political positions Friedman took have to admit that he was a great economist, who got some very important things right. Unfortunately, one of his most influential pronouncements—that the Great Depression would not have happened if the Fed had done its job, and that appropriate monetary policy could stop anything like that from happening a second time—was almost surely wrong. And this wrongness had a serious consequence: there was very little discussion, either within the Fed and its sister

institutions elsewhere or in professional research, of what policies might be used when monetary policy isn't enough.

To give you an idea of the state of mind prevailing before
the crisis, here's what Ben Bernanke said in 2002 at a conference honoring Friedman on his ninetieth birthday: "Let me
end my talk by abusing slightly my status as an official repre-
sentative of the Federal Reserve. I would like to say to Milton
and Anna: Regarding the Great Depression. You're right, we
did it. We're very sorry. But thanks to you, we won't do it
again."

What actually happened, of course, was that in 2008–09
the Fed did everything Friedman said it should have done in
the 1930s—and even so the economy seems trapped in a syn-
drome that, while not nearly as bad as the Great Depression,
bears a clear family resemblance. Moreover, many economists,
far from being ready to help craft and defend additional steps,
raised extra barriers to action instead.

What was striking and disheartening about these barriers to
action was—there's no other way to say it—the sheer ignorance
they displayed. Remember how, in chapter 2, I quoted Brian
Riedl of the Heritage Foundation to illustrate the fallacy of
Say's Law, the belief that income is necessarily spent and supply
creates its own demand? Well, in early 2009 two influential
economists from the University of Chicago, Eugene Fama and
John Cochrane, made exactly the same argument for why fiscal stimulus couldn't do any good—and presented this long-
refuted fallacy as a deep insight that Keynesian economists had
somehow failed to grasp over the past three generations.

Nor was this the only argument from ignorance presented
against stimulus. For example, Harvard's Robert Barro argued
that much of the stimulus would be offset by a fall in pri-

vate consumption and investment, which he helpfully noted is what happened when federal spending soared during World War II. Apparently nobody suggested to him that consumer spending might have fallen during the war because there was, you know, rationing, or that investment spending might have fallen because the government temporarily banned nonessential construction. Robert Lucas meanwhile argued that stimulus would be ineffective on the basis of a principle known as "Ricardian equivalence"—and in the process demonstrated that he either didn't know or had forgotten how that principle actually works.

Just as a side note, many of the economists coming out with these things tried to pull rank on those arguing for stimulus. Cochrane, for example, declared that stimulus was "not part of what anybody has taught graduate students since the 1960s. They [Keynesian ideas] are fairy tales that have been proved false. It is very comforting in times of stress to go back to the fairy tales we heard as children, but it doesn't make them less false."

Meanwhile, Lucas dismissed the analysis of Christina Romer, Obama's chief economic adviser and a distinguished student of (among other things) the Great Depression, as "schlock economics," and accused her of pandering, offering a "naked rationalization for policies that, you know, were already decided on for other reasons."

And yes, Barro tried to suggest that I personally wasn't qualified to comment on macroeconomics.

In case you're wondering, all the economists I've just mentioned are political conservatives. So to some extent these economists were in effect acting as spear-carriers for the Republican Party. But they wouldn't have been quite so willing to say such things, and wouldn't have made so many demonstrations of ignorance, if the profession as a whole hadn't lost its way so badly over the preceding three decades.

Just to be clear, there were some economists who had never forgotten about the Great Depression and its implications, Christy Romer among them. And at this point, in the fourth year of the crisis, there is a growing body of excellent work, much of it by young economists, on fiscal policy—work that by and large confirms that fiscal stimulus is effective, and implicitly suggests that it should have been done on a much larger scale.

But at the decisive moment, when what we really needed was clarity, economists presented a cacophony of views, undermining rather than reinforcing the case for action.

CHAPTER SEVEN

ANATOMY OF AN INADEQUATE RESPONSE

I see the following scenario: a weak stimulus plan, perhaps even weaker than what we're talking about now, is crafted to win those extra GOP votes. The plan limits the rise in unemployment, but things are still pretty bad, with the rate peaking at something like 9 percent and coming down only slowly. And then Mitch McConnell says "See, government spending doesn't work."

Let's hope I've got this wrong.

—From my blog, January 6, 2009

BARACK OBAMA WAS sworn in as president of the United States on January 20, 2009. His inaugural address acknowledged the dire state of the economy, but promised "action, bold and swift," to end the crisis. And his actions were indeed swift—swift enough that by the summer of 2009 the economy's free fall had ended.

But they were not bold. The centerpiece of Obama's economic strategy, the American Recovery and Reinvestment Act, was the biggest job-creation program in U.S. history—but it was also woefully inadequate to the task. Nor is this a case of twenty-twenty hindsight. In January 2009, as the out-

lines of the plan became visible, sympathetic economists outside the administration were very publicly worried about what
they feared would be the economic and political consequences
of the half measures being contemplated; we know now that
some economists inside the administration, including Christina Romer, the head of the Council of Economic Advisers,
shared these sentiments.

To be fair to Obama, his failure was more or less paral-
leled throughout the advanced world, as policy makers everywhere fell short. Governments and central banks stepped in
with cheap-money policies and enough aid to the banks to
prevent a repeat of the wholesale breakdown of finance that
took place in the early 1930s, creating a three-year credit
crunch that played a major role in causing the Great Depression. (There was a similar credit crunch in 2008–09, but it was
much shorter-lived, lasting only from September 2008 to the
late spring of 2009.) But policies were never remotely strong
enough to avoid a huge and persistent rise in unemployment.
And when the initial round of policy responses fell short, governments across the advanced world, far from acknowledging
the shortfall, treated it as a demonstration that nothing more
could or should be done to create jobs.

So policy failed to rise to the occasion. How did this
happen?

On one side, those who had more or less the right ideas
about what the economy needed, including President Obama,
were timid, never willing either to acknowledge just how
much action was required or to admit later on that what they
did in the first round was inadequate. On the other, people
with the wrong ideas—both conservative politicians and the
freshwater economists I talked about in chapter 6—were vehe-

ment and untroubled by self-doubt. Even in the dire winter of 2008–09, when one might have expected them to at least consider the possibility that they were wrong, they were ferocious in their efforts to block anything that went counter to their ideology. Those who were right lacked all conviction, while those who were wrong were filled with a passionate intensity.

In what follows, I'm going to focus on the U.S. experience, with just a few nods to events elsewhere. Partly that's because the American story is the one I know best and, frankly, care about most; but it's also because developments in Europe had a special character, thanks to the problems of Europe's shared currency, and need a treatment all their own.

So without further ado, let's turn to the story of how the crisis unfolded, and then to those fateful months in late 2008 and early 2009 when policy fell decisively and disastrously short.

The Crisis Arrives

America's Minsky moment wasn't actually a moment; it was a process that stretched over more than two years, with the pace picking up dramatically toward the end. First, the great housing bubble of the Bush years began to deflate. Then losses on financial instruments backed by mortgages began to take a toll on financial institutions. Then matters came to a head with the failure of Lehman Brothers, which triggered a general run on the "shadow banking" system. At that point bold, drastic policy actions, actions that went beyond just putting out the fires, were called for—and weren't delivered.

By the summer of 2005 home prices in the major cities of the "sand states"—Florida, Arizona, Nevada, and California— were roughly 150 percent higher than they had been at the beginning of the decade. Other cities saw smaller increases, but there had clearly been a national home price boom that bore all the signs of a classic bubble: belief that prices never go down, a rush by buyers to get in before prices went still higher, and lots of speculative activity; there was even a reality-TV show named *Flip This House*. Yet the bubble was already starting to leak air; prices were still rising in most places, but houses were taking much longer to sell.

According to the widely used Case-Shiller index, home prices nationally peaked in the spring of 2006. In the years that followed, the widespread belief that home prices never go down was brutally refuted. The cities that had the biggest price increases during the bubble years saw the biggest declines: around 50 percent in Miami, almost 60 percent in Las Vegas.

Somewhat surprisingly, the popping of the housing bubble didn't lead to an immediate recession. Home construction fell sharply, but for a while the decline in construction was offset by a boom in exports, the fruit of a weak dollar that made U.S. manufacturing very competitive on costs. By the summer of 2007, however, the troubles of housing began turning into troubles for the banks, which began suffering large losses on mortgage-backed securities—financial instruments created by selling claims on the payments from a number of pooled mortgages, with some of those claims being senior to others, that is, having first dibs on the money coming in.

These senior claims were supposed to be very low-risk; after all, how likely was it that a large number of people would default on their mortgages at the same time? The answer, of course, is that it was quite likely in an environment where homes were worth 30, 40, 50 percent less than the borrowers originally paid for them. So a lot of supposedly safe assets, assets that had been rated AAA by Standard & Poor's or Moody's, ended up becoming "toxic waste," worth only a fraction of their face value. Some of that toxic waste had been unloaded on unwary buyers, like the Florida teachers' retirement system. But much of it had stayed within the financial system, bought by banks or shadow banks. And since both conventional and shadow banks are highly leveraged, it didn't take a lot of losses on this scale to call the solvency of many institutions into question.

The seriousness of the situation began to sink in on August 9, 2007, when the French investment bank BNP Paribas told investors in two of its funds that they could no longer withdraw their money, because the markets in those assets had effectively shut down. A credit crunch began developing, as banks, worried about possible losses, became unwilling to lend to one another. The combined effects of the decline in home construction, weakening consumer spending as the fall in home prices took its toll, and this credit crunch pushed the U.S. economy into recession by the end of 2007.

At first, however, it wasn't that steep a downturn, and as late as September 2008 it was possible to hope that the economic downturn wouldn't be all that severe. In fact, there were many who argued that America wasn't really in recession. Remember Phil Gramm, the former senator who engineered the repeal of Glass-Steagall, then went to work for the financial industry? In 2008 he was an adviser to John McCain, the Republican presidential candidate, and in July of that year he declared that we were only in a "mental recession," not a real recession. He continued, "We have sort of become a nation of whiners."

In reality, a definite downturn was under way, with the unemployment rate already up from 4.7 percent to 5.8 percent. But it was true that the real awfulness still lay in the future; the economy wouldn't go into free fall until the failure of Lehman Brothers, on September 15, 2008.

Why did the failure of what was, in the end, only a medium-sized investment bank do so much harm? The immediate answer is that Lehman's fall triggered a run on the shadow banking system, and in particular on the particular form of shadow banking known as "repo." Recall from chapter 4 that repo is a system in which financial players like Lehman fund their investments by getting very short-term loans—often overnight—from other players, putting up assets like mortgage-backed securities as collateral. It's just a form of banking, because players like Lehman had long-term assets (like mortgage-backed securities) but short-term liabilities (repo). But it was banking without any safeguards like deposit insurance. And firms like Lehman were very lightly regulated, which meant that they typically borrowed up to the hilt, with debts almost as large as their assets. All it would take was a bit of bad news, such as a sharp fall in the value of mortgage-backed securities, to put them underwater.

Repo was, in short, extremely vulnerable to the twenty-first-century version of a bank run. And that's what happened in the fall of 2008. Lenders who had previously been willing to roll over their loans to the likes of Lehman no longer trusted the other side to make good on its promise to buy back the securities it temporarily sold, so they began requiring extra security in the form of "haircuts"—basically putting up extra assets as collateral. Since investment banks had limited assets, however, this meant that they could no longer borrow enough to meet their cash needs; they therefore began frantically sell-

ing assets, which drove prices lower and made lenders demand
even bigger haircuts.

Within days of Lehman's failure, this modern version of a
bank run had wreaked havoc not just with the financial system
but with the financing of real activity. The very safest borrowers—the U.S. government, of course, and major corporations
with solid bottom lines—were still able to borrow at fairly
low rates. But borrowers who looked even slightly risky were
either shut out of borrowing or forced to pay very high interest
rates. The figure below shows yields on "high-yield" corporate securities, aka junk bonds, which were paying less than 8
percent before the crisis; this rate shot up to 23 percent after
Lehman fell.

The Lehman Effect: High-Yield Corporate Bonds

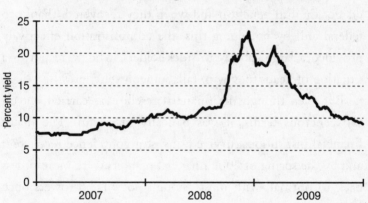

Interest rates on all but the safest assets soared after Lehman failed on September 15, 2008, helping to send the economy into a nosedive.

Source: Federal Reserve Bank of St. Louis

The prospect of a complete meltdown of the financial system concentrated the minds of policy makers—and when it
came to saving the banks, they acted strongly and decisively.

The Federal Reserve made huge loans to banks and other financial institutions, ensuring that they didn't run out of cash. It also created an alphabet soup of special lending arrangements to fill the funding holes left by the crippled state of the banks. After two tries, the Bush administration got the Troubled Asset Relief Program (TARP) through Congress, creating a $700 billion bailout fund that was used mainly to buy stakes in banks, making them better capitalized.

There's a lot to criticize about the way this financial bailout was handled. The banks did need to be rescued, but the government should have struck a much harder bargain, demanding a larger stake in return for emergency aid. At the time, I urged the Obama administration to take Citigroup and possibly a few other banks into receivership, not in order to run them on a long-term basis but in order to ensure that taxpayers got the full benefit if and when they recovered, thanks to federal aid; by not doing this, the administration effectively provided a large subsidy to stockholders, who were put in a situation of heads they win, tails someone else loses.

But even though the financial rescue was carried out on too-generous terms, it was basically successful. The major financial institutions survived; investor confidence recovered; and by the spring of 2009 financial markets were more or less back to normal, with most, though not all, borrowers once again able to raise money at fairly reasonable interest rates.

Unfortunately, that wasn't enough. You can't have prosperity without a functioning financial system, but stabilizing the financial system doesn't necessarily yield prosperity. What America needed was a rescue plan for the real economy of production and jobs that was as forceful and adequate to the task as the financial rescue. What America actually got fell far short of that goal.

Inadequate Stimulus

By December 2008, members of Barack Obama's transition team were preparing to take over management of the U.S. economy. It was already clear that they faced a very scary prospect. Falling home and stock prices had delivered a body blow to wealth; household net worth fell $13 trillion—an amount roughly equal to a year's worth of production of goods and services—over the course of 2008. Consumer spending naturally fell off a cliff, and business spending, which was also suffering from the effects of the credit crunch, followed, since there's no reason to expand a business whose customers have disappeared.

So what was to be done? The usual first line of defense against recessions is the Federal Reserve, which normally cuts interest rates when the economy stumbles. But short-term interest rates, which are what the Fed normally controls, were already zero and couldn't be cut further.

That left, as the obvious answer, fiscal stimulus—temporary increases in government spending and/or tax cuts, designed to support overall spending and create jobs. And the Obama administration did in fact design and enact a stimulus bill, the American Recovery and Reinvestment Act. Unfortunately, the bill, clocking in at $787 billion, was far too small for the job. It surely mitigated the recession, but it fell far short of what would have been needed to restore full employment, or even to create a sense of progress. Worse yet, the failure of the stimulus to deliver clear success had the effect, in the minds of voters, of discrediting the whole concept of using government spending to create jobs. So the Obama administration didn't get a chance for a do-over.

Before I get to the reasons why the stimulus was so inadequate, let me respond to two objections people like me often encounter. First is the claim that we're just making excuses, that this is all an after-the-fact attempt to rationalize the failure of our preferred policy. Second is the declaration that Obama has presided over a huge expansion of government, so it can't be right to say that he spent too little.

The answer to the first claim is that this *isn't* after the fact: many economists warned from the beginning that the administration's proposal was woefully inadequate. For example, the day after the stimulus was signed, Columbia's Joseph Stiglitz (a Nobel laureate in economics) declared,

> I think there is a broad consensus but not universal among economists that the stimulus package that was passed was badly designed and not enough. I know it is not universal but let me try to explain. First of all that it was not enough should be pretty apparent from what I just said: It is trying to offset the deficiency in aggregate demand and it is just too small.

I personally was more or less tearing my hair out in public as the shape of the administration's plan began to come clear. I wrote,

> Bit by bit we're getting information on the Obama stimulus plan, enough to start making back-of-the-envelope estimates of impact. The bottom line is this: we're probably looking at a plan that will shave less than 2 percentage points off the average unemployment rate for the next two years, and possibly quite a lot less.

After going through the math, I concluded with the statement quoted at the beginning of this chapter, in which I feared that an inadequate stimulus would both fail to produce adequate recovery and undermine the political case for further action.

Unfortunately, neither Stiglitz nor I was wrong in our fears. Unemployment peaked even higher than I expected, at more than 10 percent, but the basic shape of both the economic outcome and its political implications was just as I feared. And as you can clearly see, we were warning about the inadequacy of the stimulus right from the beginning, not making excuses after the fact.

What about the vast expansion of government that has supposedly taken place under Obama? Well, federal spending as a percentage of GDP has indeed risen, from 19.7 percent of GDP in fiscal 2007 to 24.1 percent in fiscal 2011. (Fiscal years begin on October 1 of the preceding calendar year.) But this rise doesn't mean what many people think it means. Why not?

First of all, one reason the ratio of spending to GDP is high is that GDP is low. On the basis of previous trends, we should have expected the U.S. economy to grow around 9 percent over the four years from 2007 to 2011. In fact, it barely grew at all, as a steep slump from 2007 to 2009 was followed by a weak recovery that by 2011 had only just made up the lost ground. So even normal growth in federal spending would have produced a sharp rise in spending as a share of GDP, simply because GDP growth was far below its normal trend.

That said, there was exceptionally rapid growth in federal spending from 2007 to 2011. But this didn't represent a huge expansion of the government's operations; the higher spending was overwhelmingly about emergency aid for Americans in need.

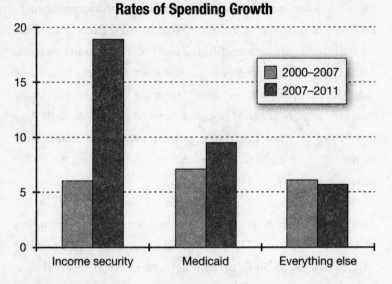

Rates of Spending Growth

Spending did rise faster than usual, but all of the difference was due to an expansion of safety-net programs in response to the economic emergency.

Source: Congressional Budget Office

The figure above illustrates what really happened, using data from the Congressional Budget Office. The CBO divides spending into a number of categories; I've broken out two of these categories, "income security" and Medicaid, and compared them with everything else. For each category I've compared the rate of growth in spending from 2000 to 2007—that is, between two periods of more or less full employment, under a conservative Republican administration—with the growth from 2007 to 2011, amid economic crisis.

Now, "income security" is mainly unemployment benefits, food stamps, and the earned-income tax credit, which helps the working poor. That is, it consists of programs that help poor or near-poor Americans, and which you'd expect to spend more if the number of Americans in financial distress rises. Meanwhile, Medicaid is also a means-tested program to help the poor and near-poor, so it also should spend more if the nation is experiencing hard times. What we can see right away from the figure is that *all* of the acceleration in spending growth can be attributed to programs that were basically emergency aid to those suffering distress from the recession. So much for the notion that Obama engaged in a huge expansion of government.

So what did Obama do? The American Recovery and Reinvestment Act (ARRA), the official name for the stimulus plan, had a headline price tag of $787 billion, although some of that was tax cuts that would have taken place anyway. Indeed, almost 40 percent of the total consisted of tax cuts, which were probably only half or less as effective in stimulating demand as actual increases in government spending.

Of the rest, a large chunk consisted of funds to extend unemployment benefits, another chunk consisted of aid to help sustain Medicaid, and a further chunk was aid to state and local governments to help them avoid spending cuts as their revenues fell. Only a fairly small piece was for the kind of spending—building and fixing roads, and so on—that we normally think of when we talk of stimulus. There was nothing resembling an FDR-style Works Progress Administration. (At its peak, the WPA employed three million Americans, or about 10 percent of the workforce. An equivalent-sized program today would employ thirteen million workers.)

Still, almost $800 billion sounds to most people like a lot of money. How did those of us who took the numbers seriously know that it was grossly inadequate? The answer is twofold: history plus an appreciation of just how big the U.S. economy is.

History told us that the slumps that follow a financial crisis are usually nasty, brutish, and long. For example, Sweden
had a banking crisis in 1990; even though the government
stepped in to bail out the banks, the crisis was followed by
an economic slump that drove real (inflation-adjusted) GDP
down by 4 percent, and the economy didn't regain its precrisis
level of GDP until 1994. There was every reason to believe
that the U.S. experience would be at least as bad, among other
things because Sweden could alleviate its slump by exporting
to less troubled economies, whereas in 2009 America had to
deal with a global crisis. So a realistic assessment was that the
stimulus would have to deal with three or more years of severe
economic pain.

And the U.S. economy is really, really big, producing close
to $15 trillion worth of goods and services every year. Think
about that: if the U.S. economy was going to experience a
three-year crisis, the stimulus was trying to rescue a $45 tril-
lion economy—the value of output over three years—with a
$787 billion plan, amounting to well under 2 percent of the
economy's total spending over that period. Suddenly $787 bil-
lion doesn't seem like that much, does it?

One more thing: the stimulus plan was designed to give
a relatively short-term boost to the economy, not long-term
support. The ARRA had its maximum positive impact on the
economy in the middle of 2010, then began fading out fairly
rapidly. This would have been OK for a short-term slump,
but given the prospect of a much longer-term blow to the
economy—which is more or less what always happens after a
financial crisis—it was a recipe for grief.

This all raises the question, why was the plan so inadequate?

Reasons Why

Let me say right away that I don't intend to spend much time revisiting the decisions of early 2009, which are water under the bridge at this point. This book is about what to do *now*, not about placing blame for what was done wrong in the past. Still, I can't avoid a brief discussion of how the Obama administration, despite being Keynesian in principle, fell vastly short in its immediate response to the crisis.

There are two competing theories about why the Obama stimulus was so inadequate. One emphasizes the political limits; according to this theory, Obama got all he could. The other argues that the administration failed to grasp the severity of the crisis, and also failed to appreciate the political fallout from an inadequate plan. My own take is that the politics of adequate stimulus were very hard, but we will never know whether they really prevented an adequate plan, because Obama and his aides never even tried for something big enough to do the job.

There's no doubt that the political environment was very difficult, largely because of the rules of the U.S. Senate, in which 60 votes are normally needed to override a filibuster. Obama seems to have arrived in office expecting bipartisan support for his efforts to rescue the economy; he was completely wrong. From day one, Republicans offered scorched-earth opposition to anything and everything he proposed. In the end, he was able to get his 60 votes by winning over three moderate Republican senators, but they demanded, as the price of their support, that he slash $100 billion in aid to state and local governments from the bill.

Many commentators see that demand for a smaller stimulus as a clear demonstration that no bigger bill was possible. I guess I don't think of it as being all that clear. First of all, there may have been a pound-of-flesh aspect to the behavior of those three senators: they had to make a show of cutting something to prove that they weren't giving away the store. So you can make a reasonable case that the real limit on stimulus wasn't $787 billion, that it was $100 billion less than Obama's plan, whatever it was; if he had asked for more, he wouldn't have gotten all he asked for, but he would have gotten a bigger effort all the same.

Also, there was available an alternative to wooing those three Republicans: Obama could have passed a bigger stimulus by using reconciliation, a parliamentary procedure that bypasses the threat of a filibuster and therefore reduces the number of Senate votes needed to 50 (because in the case of a tie the vice president can cast the deciding vote). In 2010 Democrats would in fact use reconciliation to pass health reform. Nor would this have been an extreme tactic by historical standards: both rounds of Bush tax cuts, in 2001 and 2003, were passed by means of reconciliation, and the 2003 round in fact gained only 50 votes in the Senate, with Dick Cheney casting the decisive vote.

There's another problem with the claim that Obama obtained all he could: he and his administration never made the case that they would have liked a bigger bill. On the contrary, when the bill was before the Senate, the president declared that "broadly speaking, the plan is the right size. It is the right scope." And to this day administration officials like to claim not that the plan was undersized because of Republican opposition but that at the time nobody realized that a much bigger plan was needed. As late as December 2011, Jay Carney, the White House press secretary, was saying things like this: "There was not a single mainstream, Wall Street, academic economist who knew at the time, in January of 2009, just how deep the economic hole was that we were in."

As we've already seen, that was not at all the case. So what did happen?

Ryan Lizza of *The New Yorker* has acquired and made public the memo on economic policy that Larry Summers, who would soon be the administration's top economist, prepared for President-elect Obama in December 2008. This fifty-seven-page document quite clearly had multiple authors, not all of them on the same page. But there is a telling passage (on page 11) laying out the case against too big a package. Three main points emerge:

1. "An excessive recovery package could spook markets or the public and be counterproductive."
2. "The economy can only absorb so much 'priority investment' over the next two years."
3. "It is easier to add down the road to insufficient fiscal stimulus than to subtract from excessive fiscal stimulus. We can if necessary take further steps."

Of these, point 1 involves invoking the threat of "bond vigilantes," of which more in the next chapter; suffice it to say that this fear has proved unjustified. Point 2 was clearly right, but it's unclear why it precluded more aid to state and local governments. In his remarks just after the ARRA was passed, Joe Stiglitz noted that it provided "a little of federal aid but just not enough. So what we will be doing is we will be laying off teachers and laying off people in the health care sector while we are hiring construction workers. It is a little strange for a design of a stimulus package."

Also, given the likelihood of a prolonged slump, why the two-year limit on the horizon?

Finally, point 3, about the ability to go back for more, was totally wrong—and obviously so, at least to me, even at the time. So there was a major political misjudgment on the part of the economic team.

For a variety of reasons, then, the Obama administration did the right thing but on a wholly inadequate scale. As we'll see later, there was a similar shortfall in Europe, for somewhat different reasons.

Housing Fiasco

So far I've talked about the inadequacy of fiscal stimulus. But a big failure occurred on another front, too—mortgage relief.

I've argued that high levels of household debt were a major reason the economy was vulnerable to crisis, and that a key to the continuing weakness of the U.S. economy is the fact that households are trying to pay down debt by spending less, with nobody else willing to spend more to compensate. The case for fiscal policy is precisely that by spending more the government can keep the economy from being deeply depressed while indebted families restore their own financial health.

But this story also suggests an alternative or, better yet, complementary road to recovery: just reduce the debt directly. Debt, after all, isn't a physical object—it's a contract, something written on paper and enforced by government. So why not rewrite the contracts?

And don't say that contracts are sacred, never to be rene-gotiated. Orderly bankruptcy, which reduces debts when they simply cannot be paid, is a long-established part of our economic system. Corporations routinely, and often voluntarily, enter Chapter 11, in which they remain in business but are able to rewrite and mark down some of their obligations. (As this chapter was being written, American Airlines voluntarily entered bankruptcy to get out of costly union contracts.) Individuals can declare bankruptcy, too, and the settlement usually relieves them of some debts.

Home mortgages, however, have historically been treated differently from things like credit card debt. The assumption has always been that the first thing that happens when a family can't make mortgage payments is that it loses the house; that ends the matter in some states, while in others the lender can still go after the borrower if the house isn't worth as much as the mortgage. In either case, however, homeowners who can't make their payments face foreclosure. And maybe that's a good system in normal times, in part because people who can't make their mortgage payments usually sell their houses rather than waiting for foreclosure.

These are not, however, normal times. Normally, only a relatively small number of homeowners are underwater, that is, owe more than their houses are currently worth. The great housing bubble and its deflation, however, have left more than ten million homeowners—more than one in five mortgages—underwater, even as the continuing economic slump leaves many families with only a fraction of their previous income. So there are many people who can neither make their payments nor pay off their mortgage by selling the house, a recipe for an epidemic of foreclosures.

And foreclosure is a terrible deal for all concerned. The homeowner, of course, loses the house; but the lender rarely

does well out of the deal, both because it's an expensive procedure and because banks are trying to sell foreclosed homes in a
terrible market. It would seemingly be beneficial to both sides
to have a program that offers troubled borrowers some relief
while sparing lenders the costs of foreclosure. There would be
benefits to third parties as well: locally, empty foreclosed properties are a blight on the neighborhood, while nationally, debt
relief would help the macroeconomic situation.

So everything would seem to call for a program of debt
relief, and the Obama administration did in fact announce
such a program in 2009. But the whole effort has turned into
a sick joke: very few borrowers have gotten significant relief,
and some have actually found themselves deeper in debt thanks
to the program's Kafkaesque rules and functioning.

What went wrong? The details are complex, and mind-
numbing. But a capsule summary would be that the Obama
administration never had its heart in the program, that officials believed until well into the game that all would be well
if they stabilized the banks. Furthermore, they were terrified
that right-wingers would criticize the program as a giveaway
to the undeserving, that it would reward people who acted
irresponsibly; as a result, the program was so careful to avoid
any appearance of a giveaway that it ended up being more or
less unusable.

So here was another area where policy utterly failed to rise
to the occasion.

The Road Not Taken

Historically, financial crises have typically been followed by
prolonged economic slumps, and U.S. experience since 2007
has been no different. Indeed, U.S. numbers on unemployment

and growth have been remarkably close to the historical average for countries experiencing these kinds of problems. Just as the crisis was gathering momentum, Carmen Reinhart, of the Peterson Institute of International Economics, and Kenneth Rogoff, of Harvard, published a history of financial crises with the ironic title *This Time Is Different* (because in reality it never is). Their research led readers to expect a protracted period of high unemployment, and as the story unfolded, Rogoff would note that America was experiencing a "garden-variety severe financial crisis."

But it didn't have to be like this, and it doesn't have to stay like this. There were things policy makers could have done at any point in the past three years that would have greatly improved the situation. Politics and intellectual confusion—not fundamental economic realities—blocked effective action.

And the road out of depression and back to full employment is still wide open. We don't have to suffer like this.

CHAPTER EIGHT

BUT WHAT ABOUT
THE DEFICIT?

There may be some tax provisions that can encourage businesses to hire sooner rather than sitting on the sidelines. So we're taking a look at those.

I think it is important, though, to recognize if we keep on adding to the debt, even in the midst of this recovery, that at some point, people could lose confidence in the U.S. economy in a way that could actually lead to a double-dip recession.

—President Barack Obama, on Fox News, November 2009

BY THE FALL OF 2009 it was already obvious that those who had warned that the original stimulus plan was much too small had been right. True, the economy was no longer in free fall. But the decline had been steep, and there were no signs of a recovery fast enough to bring unemployment down at anything more than a glacial pace.

This was exactly the kind of situation in which White House aides had originally envisaged going back to Congress for more stimulus. But that didn't happen. Why not?

One reason was that they had misjudged the politics: just as some had feared when the original plan came out, the inadequacy of the first stimulus had discredited the whole notion of stimulus in the minds of most Americans and had emboldened Republicans in their scorched-earth opposition.

There was, however, another reason: much of the discussion in Washington had shifted from a focus on unemployment to a focus on debt and deficits. Ominous warnings about the danger of excessive deficits became a staple of political posturing; they were used by people who considered themselves serious to proclaim their seriousness. As the opening quotation makes clear, Obama himself got into this game; his first State of the Union address, in early 2010, proposed spending cuts rather than new stimulus. And by 2011 blood-curdling warnings of disaster unless we dealt with deficits immediately (as opposed to taking longer-term measures that wouldn't depress the economy further) were heard across the land.

The strange thing is that there was and is no evidence to support the shift in focus away from jobs and toward deficits. Where the harm done by lack of jobs is real and terrible, the harm done by deficits to a nation like America in its current situation is, for the most part, hypothetical. The quantifiable burden of debt is much smaller than you would imagine from the rhetoric, and warnings about some kind of debt crisis are based on nothing much at all. In fact, the predictions of deficit hawks have been repeatedly falsified by events, while those who argued that deficits are not a problem in a depressed economy have been consistently right. Furthermore, those who made investment decisions based on the predictions of the deficit alarmists, like Morgan Stanley in 2010 or Pimco in 2011, ended up losing a lot of money.

Yet exaggerated fear of deficits retains its hold on our political and policy discourse. I'll try to explain why later in this chapter. First, however, let me talk about what deficit hawks have said, and what has really happened.

Invisible Bond Vigilantes

I used to think if there was reincarnation, I wanted to come back as the President or the Pope or a .400 baseball hitter. But now I want to come back as the bond market. You can intimidate everyone.
—James Carville, Clinton campaign strategist

Back in the 1980s the business economist Ed Yardeni coined the term "bond vigilantes" for investors who dump a country's bonds—driving up its borrowing costs—when they lose confidence in its monetary and/or fiscal policies. Fear of budget deficits is driven mainly by fear of an attack by the bond vigilantes. And advocates of fiscal austerity, of sharp cuts in government spending even in the face of mass unemployment, often argue that we must do what they demand to satisfy the bond market.

But the market itself doesn't seem to agree; if anything, it's saying that America should borrow more, since at the moment U.S. borrowing costs are very low. In fact, adjusted for inflation, they're actually negative, so that investors are in effect paying the U.S. government a fee to keep their wealth safe. Oh, and these are long-term interest rates, so the market isn't just saying that things are OK now; it's saying that investors don't see any major problems for years to come.

Never mind, say the deficit hawks, borrowing costs will shoot up soon if we don't slash spending right now. This amounts to saying that the market is wrong—which is something you're allowed to do. But it's strange, to say the least, to base your demands on the claim that policy must be changed to satisfy the market, then dismiss the clear evidence that the market itself doesn't share your concerns.

The failure of rates to rise didn't reflect any early end to large deficits: over the course of 2008, 2009, 2010, and 2011 the combination of low tax receipts and emergency spending—both the results of a depressed economy—forced the federal government to borrow more than $5 trillion. And at every uptick in rates over that period, influential voices announced that the bond vigilantes had arrived, that America was about to find itself unable to keep on borrowing so much money. Yet each of those upticks was reversed, and at the beginning of 2012 U.S. borrowing costs were close to an all-time low.

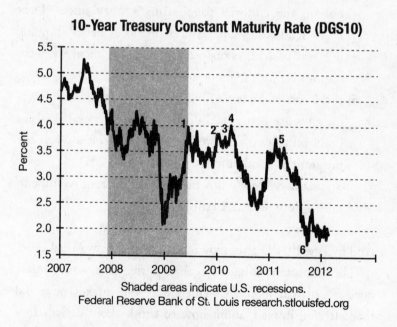

10-Year Treasury Constant Maturity Rate (DGS10)

Shaded areas indicate U.S. recessions.
Federal Reserve Bank of St. Louis research.stlouisfed.org

Source: Board of Governors of the Federal Reserve System

The figure above shows U.S. ten-year interest rates since the beginning of 2007, along with supposed sightings of those elusive bond vigilantes. Here's what the numbers on the chart refer to:

1. The *Wall Street Journal* runs an editorial titled "The Bond Vigilantes: The Disciplinarians of U.S. Policy Return," predicting that interest rates will go way up unless deficits are reduced.
2. President Obama tells Fox News that we might have a double-dip recession if we keep adding to debt.
3. Morgan Stanley predicts that deficits will drive ten-year rates up to 5.5 percent by the end of 2010.
4. The *Wall Street Journal*—this time in the news section, not on the editorial page—runs a story titled "Debt Fears Send Rates Up." It presents no evidence showing that fear of debt, as opposed to hopes for recovery, were responsible for the modest rise in rates.
5. Bill Gross of the bond fund Pimco warns that U.S. interest rates are being held down only by Federal Reserve bond purchases, and predicts a spike in rates when the program of bond purchases ends in June 2011.
6. Standard & Poor's downgrades the U.S. government, taking away its AAA rating.

And by late 2011 U.S. borrowing costs were lower than ever.

The important thing to realize is that this wasn't just a question of bad forecasts, which everyone makes now and then. It was, instead, about how to think about deficits in a depressed economy. So let's talk about why many people sincerely believed that government borrowing would send interest rates soaring, and why Keynesian economics predicted, correctly, that this wouldn't happen as long as the economy remained depressed.

Understanding Interest Rates

You can't be a monetarist and a Keynesian simultaneously—at least I can't see how you can, because if the aim of the monetarist policy is to keep interest rates down, to keep liquidity high, the effect of the Keynesian policy must be to drive interest rates up.

After all, $1.75 trillion is an awful lot of freshly minted treasuries to land on the bond market at a time of recession, and I still don't quite know who is going to buy them. It's certainly not going to be the Chinese. That worked fine in the good times, but what I call "Chimerica," the marriage between China and America, is coming to an end. Maybe it's going to end in a messy divorce.

No, the problem is that only the Fed can buy these freshly minted treasuries, and there is going to be, I predict, in the weeks and months ahead, a very painful tug-of-war between our monetary policy and our fiscal policy as the markets realize just what a vast quantity of bonds are going to have to be absorbed by the financial system this year. That will tend to drive the price of the bonds down, and drive up interest rates, which will also have an effect on mortgage rates—the precise opposite of what Ben Bernanke is trying to achieve at the Fed.

—Niall Ferguson, April 2009

This quotation from Niall Ferguson, a historian and popular TV guest who writes a lot about economics, expresses in compact form what many people thought and still think about government borrowing: that it must drive up interest rates, because it's an extra demand for scarce resources—in this case, loans—and this increase in demand will drive up the price. It basically boils down to the question of where the money is coming from.

This is, in fact, a sensible question to ask when the economy is at more or less full employment. But even then it makes no sense to argue that deficit spending actually works against monetary policy, which is what Ferguson seemed to claim. And it's very much the wrong question to ask when the economy is depressed even though the Fed has cut the interest rates it can control all the way to zero—that is, when we're in a liquidity trap, which we were in when Ferguson delivered those remarks (at a conference sponsored by PEN and the *New York Review of Books*) and which we are still in today.

Recall from chapter 2 that a liquidity trap happens when even at a zero interest rate the world's residents are collectively unwilling to buy as much stuff as they are willing to produce. Equivalently, the amount people want to save—that is, the income they don't want to spend on current consumption—is more than the amount businesses are willing to invest.

Reacting to Ferguson's remarks a couple of days later, I tried to explain this point:

> In effect, we have an incipient excess supply of savings even at a zero interest rate. And that's our problem.
>
> So what does government borrowing do? It gives some of those excess savings a place to go—and in the process expands overall demand, and hence GDP. It does NOT crowd out private spending, at least not until the excess supply of savings has been sopped up, which is the same thing as saying not until the economy has escaped from the liquidity trap.
>
> Now, there are real problems with large-scale government borrowing—mainly, the effect on the government debt burden. I don't want to minimize those problems; some countries, such as Ireland, are being forced into fiscal contraction even in the face of severe recession. But the fact remains that our current problem is, in effect, a problem of excess worldwide savings, looking for someplace to go.

The federal government has borrowed around $4 trillion since I wrote that, and interest rates have actually dropped.

Where did the money to finance all this borrowing come from? From the U.S. private sector, which reacted to the financial crisis by saving more and investing less; the financial balance of the private sector, the difference between saving and investment spending, went from −$200 billion a year before the crisis to +$1 trillion a year now.

You may ask, what would have happened if the private sector hadn't decided to save more and invest less? But the answer is, in that case the economy wouldn't have been depressed—and the government wouldn't have been running such big deficits. In short, it was just as those who understood the logic of the liquidity trap had predicted: in a depressed economy, budget deficits don't compete with the private sector for funds, and hence don't lead to soaring interest rates. The government is simply finding a use for the private sector's excess savings, that is, the excess of what it wants to save over what it is willing to invest. And it was in fact crucial that the government play this role, since without those public deficits the private sector's attempt to spend less than it earned would have caused a deep depression.

Unfortunately for the state of economic discourse, and hence for the reality of economic policy, the prophets of fiscal doom refused to take no for an answer. For the past three years they have advanced one excuse after another for the failure of interest rates to skyrocket—It's the Fed buying debt! No, it's the troubles in Europe! And so on—while steadfastly refusing to admit that they just had the wrong economic analysis.

Before going further, let me address one question that some readers may have been asking about the figure on page 133: what caused the interest rate fluctuations you see in that chart?

The answer lies in the distinction between short-term and

long-term interest rates. Short-term rates are what the Fed can control, and they have been close to zero since late 2008 (at the time of writing, the interest rate on three-month Treasury bills was 0.01 percent). But many borrowers, including the federal government, want to lock in a rate over a longer term, and nobody will buy, say, a ten-year bond at a zero interest rate, even if short-term rates are zero. Why? Because those rates can, and eventually will, go up again; and someone who ties up his money in a longer-term bond has to be compensated for the potential lost opportunity to get a higher yield if and when short rates rise again.

But how much compensation investors demand for tying their funds up in a long-term bond depends on how soon and how much they expect short rates to rise. And this in turn depends on the prospects for economic recovery, specifically on when investors believe the economy might emerge from the liquidity trap and do well enough that the Fed begins raising rates to head off possible inflation.

So the interest rates you see on page 133 reflect changing views about how long the economy will stay in depression. The rise in rates during the spring of 2009, which the *Wall Street Journal* saw as the coming of the bond vigilantes, was actually driven by optimism that the worst was past and that real recovery was on the way. As that hope faded, so did interest rates. A second wave of optimism sent rates up in late 2010, only to fade once again. At the time of writing, hope is in short supply—and rates are correspondingly low.

But wait, is that the whole story? It seems to work for the United States, but what about Greece or Italy? They're even further from recovery than we are, yet their interest rates have soared. Why?

A full answer will have to wait until I do an in-depth discussion of Europe, in chapter 10. But here's a brief preview.

If you read my reply to Ferguson, above, you'll note that I admitted that the overall debt burden could be a problem—not because U.S. government borrowing is going to be competing with the private sector for funds any time soon but because sufficiently high debt can call a government's solvency into question, and make investors unwilling to buy its bonds for fear of a future default. And fear of default is what lies behind the high interest rates on some European debt.

So is the United States a default risk, or likely to be seen as one any time soon? History suggests not: although U.S. deficits and debt are huge, so is the U.S. economy; relative to the size of that enormous economy, we're not as deeply in debt as a number of countries, ourselves included, have gone without setting off a bond market panic. The usual way to scale a nation's government debt is to divide it by that country's GDP, the total value of goods and services its economy produces in a year, because GDP is also, in effect, the government's tax base. The figure on page 140 shows historical levels of government debt as a percentage of GDP for the United States, the United Kingdom, and Japan; although U.S. debt has gone up a lot lately, it's still below levels we have seen ourselves in in the past, and far below levels that Britain has lived with for much of its modern history, all without ever facing an attack from bond vigilantes.

The case of Japan, whose debt has been rising since the 1990s, is also worth noting. Like the United States now, Japan has been repeatedly tagged over the past decade or more as a country facing an imminent debt crisis; yet the crisis keeps on not coming, with the interest rate on Japanese ten-year bonds

Comparative Debt as a Percentage of GDP

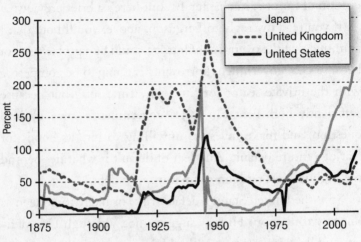

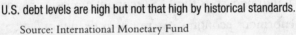

U.S. debt levels are high but not that high by historical standards.

Source: International Monetary Fund

currently around 1 percent. Investors who bet on a coming rise in Japanese interest rates lost a lot of money, to such an extent that shorting JGBs (Japanese government bonds) came to be known as the "trade of death." And those who studied Japan had a pretty good idea about what would happen when S&P downgraded the United States last year—namely, nothing—because S&P downgraded Japan back in 2002 with a similar lack of effect.

But what about Italy, Spain, Greece, and Ireland? As we'll see, none of them is as deep in debt as Britain was for much of the twentieth century, or as Japan is now, yet they definitely are facing an attack from bond vigilantes. What's the difference?

The answer, which will need a lot more explanation, is that it matters enormously whether you borrow in your own currency or in someone else's. Britain, America, and Japan all borrow in their respective currencies, the pound, the dollar, and the yen. Italy, Spain, Greece, and Ireland, by contrast, don't even have their own currencies at this point, and their debts are in euros—which, it turns out, makes them highly vulnerable to panic attacks. Much more about that later.

What about the Burden of Debt?

Suppose that the bond vigilantes aren't set to make an appearance and cause a crisis. Even so, shouldn't we be concerned about the burden of debt we're leaving for the future? The answer is a definite "Yes, but." Yes, debt we run up now, as we try to cope with the aftermath of a financial crisis, will place a burden on the future. But the burden is a lot smaller than the heated rhetoric of deficit hawks suggests.

The key thing to bear in mind is that the $5 trillion or so in debt America has run up since the crisis began, and the trillions more we'll surely run up before this economic siege is over, won't have to be paid off quickly, or indeed at all. In fact, it won't be a tragedy if the debt actually continues to grow, as long as it grows more slowly than the sum of inflation and economic growth.

To illustrate this point, consider what happened to the $241 billion in debt the U.S. government owed at the end of World War II. That doesn't sound like much by modern standards, but a dollar was worth a lot more back then and the economy was a lot smaller, so this amounted to about 120 percent of GDP (compared with a combined federal, state, and local debt of 93.5 percent of GDP at the end of 2010). How was that debt paid off? The answer is that it wasn't.

Instead, the federal government ran roughly balanced budgets over the years that followed. In 1962 the debt was about the same as it had been in 1946. But the ratio of debt to GDP had fallen 60 percent thanks to a combination of mild inflation and substantial economic growth. And the debt-to-GDP ratio kept falling through the 1960s and 1970s even though the U.S. government generally ran modest deficits in that era. It was only when the deficit got much bigger under Ronald Reagan that debt finally started growing faster than GDP.

Now let's consider what all this implies for the future burden of the debt we're building up now. We won't ever have to pay off the debt; all we'll have to do is pay enough of the interest on the debt so that the debt grows significantly more slowly than the economy.

One way to do this would be to pay enough interest so that the real value of the debt—its value adjusted for inflation—stays constant; this would mean that the ratio of debt to GDP would fall steadily as the economy grows. To do this, we'd have to pay the value of the debt multiplied by the real rate of interest—the interest rate minus inflation. And as it happens, the United States sells "inflation-protected securities" that automatically compensate for inflation; the interest rate on these bonds therefore measures the expected real rate of interest on ordinary bonds.

Right now, the real interest rate on ten-year bonds—the usual benchmark for thinking about these things—is actually slightly below zero. OK, that reflects the dire state of the economy, and that rate will rise someday. So maybe we should use the real interest rate that prevailed before the crisis, which was around 2.5 percent. How much burden would the $5 trillion in additional debt we've added since the crisis began impose if the government had to pay that much in interest?

The answer is $125 billion a year. That may sound like a big number, but in a $15 trillion economy, it's well under 1 percent of national income. The point is not that debt doesn't impose any burden at all but that even shock-and-awe debt numbers aren't nearly as big a deal as often claimed. And once you realize that, you also realize just how wrongheaded the pivot from jobs to deficits really was.

The Folly of a Short-Term Deficit Focus

When political discourse pivoted from jobs to deficits—which, as we've seen, is pretty much what happened in late 2009, with the Obama administration actually participating in the change of focus—what this translated to was both an end to proposals for further stimulus and an actual move to cut spending. Most notably, state and local governments were forced into large cutbacks as stimulus funds ran out, cutting back on public investment and laying off hundreds of thousands of teachers. And there were demands for much bigger cuts, given the persistence of large budget deficits.

Did this make any economic sense?

Think about the economic impact of cutting spending by $100 billion when the economy is in a liquidity trap—which means, again, that it remains depressed even though the interest rates the Fed can control are effectively zero, so that the Fed can't reduce rates further to offset the depressing effect of the spending cuts. Remember, spending equals income, so the decline in government purchases directly reduces GDP by $100 billion. And with lower incomes, people will cut back their own spending, too, leading to further declines in income, and more cutbacks, and so on.

OK, brief pause: some people will immediately object that lower government spending means a lower tax burden in the future. So isn't it possible that the private sector will spend more, not less? Won't cuts in government spending lead to higher confidence and perhaps even to economic expansion?

Well, influential people have made that argument, which has come to be known as the doctrine of "expansionary austerity." I'll talk about that doctrine at some length in chapter 11, in particular about how it came to have such a hold on discussion in Europe. But the bottom line is that neither the logic of the doctrine nor the alleged evidence advanced on its behalf has held up at all. Contractionary policies are, in fact, contractionary.

So let's return to the story. Slashing $100 billion in spending while we're in a liquidity trap will lead to a decline in GDP, both directly via reduced government purchases and indirectly because the weaker economy leads to private cutbacks. A lot of empirical work has been done on these effects since the coming of the crisis (some of it summarized in the postscript to this book), and it suggests that the end result will be a GDP decline of $150 billion or more.

This tells us right away that $100 billion in spending cuts won't actually reduce our future debt by $100 billion, because a weaker economy will yield less revenue (and also lead to higher spending on emergency aid programs, like food stamps and unemployment insurance). In fact, it's quite possible that the net reduction in debt will be no more than half the headline cut in spending.

Still, even that would improve the long-run fiscal picture, right? Not necessarily. The depressed state of our economy isn't just causing a lot of short-term pain, it's having a corrosive effect on our long-run prospects. Workers who have been out of a job for a long time may either lose their skills or at least start to be perceived as unemployable. Graduates who can't find jobs that use what they have learned may be permanently condemned to menial jobs despite their education. In addition, since businesses aren't expanding capacity, because of a lack of customers, the economy will run into capacity constraints sooner than it should when a real recovery finally does begin. And anything that makes the economy even more depressed will worsen these problems, reducing the economy's outlook in the long run as well as the short run.

Now think about what this means for the fiscal outlook: even if slashing spending reduces future debt, it may also reduce future income, so that the ability to bear the debt we have—as measured, say, by the ratio of debt to GDP—may actually fall. The attempt to improve the fiscal prospect by cutting spending in a depressed economy can end up being counterproductive even in narrow fiscal terms. Nor is this an outlandish possibility: serious researchers at the International Monetary Fund have looked at the evidence, and they suggest that it's a real possibility.

From a policy point of view, it doesn't really matter whether austerity in a depressed economy literally hurts a country's fiscal position or merely does very little to help that position. All that we need to know is that the payoff to fiscal cuts in times like these is small, possibly nonexistent, while the costs are large. This is really not a good time to obsess over deficits.

Yet even with all I've said, there is one rhetorically effective argument that those of us trying to fight the deficit obsession run into all the time—and have to answer.

Can Debt Cure a Problem Created by Debt?

One of the common arguments against fiscal policy in the current situation—one that sounds sensible—runs like this:

"You yourself say that this crisis is the result of too much debt. Now you're saying that the answer involves running up even more debt. That can't possibly make sense."

Actually, it does. But to explain why will take both some careful thinking and a look at the historical record.

It's true that people like me believe that the depression we're in was in large part caused by the buildup of household debt, which set the stage for a Minksy moment in which highly indebted households were forced to slash their spending. How, then, can even more debt be part of the appropriate policy response?

The key point is that this argument against deficit spending assumes, implicitly, that debt is debt—that it doesn't matter who owes the money. Yet that can't be right; if it were, we wouldn't have a problem in the first place. After all, to a first approximation debt is money we owe to ourselves; yes, the United States has debt to China and other countries, but as we saw in chapter 3, our net debt to foreigners is relatively small and not at the heart of the problem. Ignoring the foreign component, or looking at the world as a whole, we see that the overall level of debt makes no difference to aggregate net worth—one person's liability is another person's asset.

It follows that the level of debt matters only if the distribution of net worth matters, if highly indebted players face different constraints from players with low debt. And this means that all debt isn't created equal, which is why borrowing by some actors now can help cure problems created by excess borrowing by other actors in the past.

Think of it this way: when debt is rising, it's not the economy as a whole borrowing more money. It is, rather, a case of less patient people—people who for whatever reason want to spend sooner rather than later—borrowing from more patient people. The main limit on this kind of borrowing is the concern of those patient lenders about whether they will be repaid, which sets some kind of ceiling on each individual's ability to borrow.

What happened in 2008 was a sudden downward revision of those ceilings. This downward revision has forced the debtors to pay down their debt, rapidly, which means spending much less. And the problem is that the creditors don't face any equivalent incentive to spend more. Low interest rates help, but because of the severity of the "deleveraging shock," even a zero interest rate isn't low enough to get them to fill the hole left by the collapse in debtors' demand. The result isn't just a depressed economy: low incomes and low inflation (or even deflation) make it that much harder for the debtors to pay down their debt.

What can be done? One answer is to find some way to reduce the real value of the debt. Debt relief could do this; so could inflation, if you can get it, which would do two things: it would make it possible to have a negative real interest rate, and it would in itself erode the outstanding debt. Yes, that would in a way be rewarding debtors for their past excesses, but economics is not a morality play. I'll have more to say about inflation in the next chapter.

Just to go back for a moment to my point that debt is not all the same: yes, debt relief would reduce the assets of the creditors at the same time, and by the same amount, as it reduced the liabilities of the debtors. But the debtors are being forced to cut spending, while the creditors aren't, so this is a net positive for economywide spending.

But what if neither inflation nor sufficient debt relief can, or at any rate will, be delivered?

Well, suppose a third party can come in: the government.

Suppose that it can borrow for a while, using the borrowed money to buy useful things like rail tunnels under the Hudson, or pay schoolteacher salaries. The true social cost of these things will be very low, because the government will be employing resources that would otherwise be unemployed. And it also makes it easier for the debtors to pay down their debt; if the government maintains its spending long enough, it can bring debtors to the point where they're no longer being forced into emergency debt reduction and where further deficit spending is no longer required to achieve full employment.

Yes, private debt will in part have been replaced by public debt, but the point is that debt will have been shifted away from the players whose debt is doing the economic damage, so that the economy's problems will have been reduced even if the overall level of debt hasn't fallen.

The bottom line, then, is that the plausible-sounding argument that debt can't cure debt is just wrong. On the contrary, it can—and the alternative is a prolonged period of economic weakness that actually makes the debt problem harder to resolve.

OK, that's just a hypothetical story. Are there any real-world examples? Indeed there are. Consider what happened during and after World War II.

It has always been clear why World War II lifted the U.S. economy out of the Great Depression: military spending solved the problem of inadequate demand, with a vengeance. A harder question is why America didn't relapse into depression when the war was over. At the time, many people thought it would; famously, Montgomery Ward, once America's largest retailer, went into decline after the war because its CEO hoarded cash in the belief that the Depression was coming

End This Depression Now!   149

back, and it lost out to rivals who capitalized on the great postwar boom.

So why didn't the Depression come back? A likely answer is that the wartime expansion—along with a fairly substantial amount of inflation during and especially just after the war— greatly reduced the debt burden of households. Workers who earned good wages during the war, while being more or less unable to borrow, came out with much lower debt relative to income, leaving them free to borrow and spend on new houses in the suburbs. The consumer boom took over as the war spending fell back, and in the stronger postwar economy the government could in turn let growth and inflation reduce its debt relative to GDP.

In short, the government debt run up to fight the war was, in fact, the solution to a problem brought on by too much private debt. The persuasive-sounding slogan that debt can't cure a debt problem is just wrong.

Why the Deficit Obsession?

We've just seen that the "pivot" from jobs to deficits that took place in the United States (and, as we'll see, in Europe) was a big mistake. Yet deficit scaremongering took over the debate and even now retains much of its grip.

This clearly needs some explaining, and the explanation is coming. But before we get there I want to discuss another great fear that has had a powerful impact on economic discourse, even as it keeps being refuted by events: fear of inflation.

CHAPTER NINE

INFLATION:
THE PHANTOM MENACE

PAYNE: So, where are you then, Peter, with respect to inflation? Do you think this is going to be the big story of 2010?

SCHIFF: You know, look, I know inflation is going to get worse in 2010. Whether it's going to run out of control or it's going to take until 2011 or 2012, but I know we're going to have a major currency crisis coming soon. It's going to dwarf the financial crisis and it's going to send consumer prices absolutely ballistic, as well as interest rates and unemployment.

—"Austrian" economist Peter Schiff on
Glenn Beck, December 28, 2009

The Zimbabwe/Weimar Thing

For the past few years—especially, of course, since Barack Obama took office—the airwaves and opinion pages have been filled with dire warnings of high inflation just around the corner. And not just inflation: predictions abound of full-fledged hyperinflation, of America following in the footsteps of modern Zimbabwe or Weimar Germany in the 1920s.

The right side of the U.S. political spectrum has bought fully into these fears of inflation. Ron Paul, a self-proclaimed devotee of Austrian economics who routinely issues apocalyptic warnings about inflation, heads the House subcommittee on monetary policy, and the failure of his presidential aspirations should not blind us to his success in making his economic ideology Republican orthodoxy. Republican congressmen berate Ben Bernanke for "debasing" the dollar; Republican presidential candidates compete over who can denounce the Fed's allegedly inflationary policies most vehemently, with Rick Perry taking the prize by warning the Fed chairman that "we would treat him pretty ugly in Texas" if he pursued any further expansionary policies.

And it's not just the obvious cranks who have been fearmongering over inflation; conservative economists with mainstream credentials have played their part, too. Thus Allan Meltzer, a well-known monetary economist and Fed historian, took to the pages of the *New York Times* on May 3, 2009, to deliver an ominous message:

> [T]he interest rate the Fed controls is nearly zero; and the enormous increase in bank reserves—caused by the Fed's purchases of bonds and mortgages—will surely bring on severe inflation if allowed to remain. . . .
>
> [N]o country facing enormous budget deficits, rapid growth in the money supply and the prospect of a sustained currency devaluation as we are has ever experienced deflation. These factors are harbingers of inflation.

But he was wrong. Two and a half years after his warning, the interest rate the Fed controls was still near zero; the Fed had continued to buy bonds and mortgages, adding even more to bank reserves; and budget deficits remained enormous. Yet the average inflation rate over that period was only 2.5 percent, and if you excluded volatile food and energy prices—which

Meltzer himself said you should—the average inflation rate
was only 1.4 percent. These inflation rates were below historical norms. In particular, as liberal economists loved to point
out, inflation was much lower under Obama than it had been
in Ronald Reagan's supposedly halcyon, "morning in America" second term.

Furthermore, people like me knew that it would turn out
this way—that runaway inflation just wasn't going to happen as
long as the economy stayed depressed. We knew this both from
theory and from history, because the fact was that after 2000
Japan had combined large deficits with rapid money growth in
a depressed economy and, far from experiencing severe inflation, remained stuck in deflation. To be honest, I thought we
too might be facing actual deflation by now; I'll talk in the next
chapter about why that hasn't happened. Still, the prediction
that the supposedly inflationary actions of the Fed would not,
in fact, lead to higher inflation has been borne out.

Yet Meltzer's warning sounds plausible, doesn't it? With the
Fed printing lots of money—for that, roughly speaking, is how
it pays for all those bonds and mortgages it buys—and the
federal government running trillion-dollar-plus deficits, why
aren't we seeing a sharp rise in inflation?

The answer lies in depression economics, specifically in
what I hope has become the familiar concept of the liquidity
trap, in which even zero interest rates aren't low enough to
induce sufficient spending to restore full employment. When
you're *not* in a liquidity trap, printing lots of money is indeed
inflationary. But when you are in one, it isn't; in fact, the
amount of money the Fed prints is very nearly irrelevant.

Let's talk basic concepts for a moment, then look at what
has actually happened.

Money, Demand, and Inflation (or Lack Thereof)

Everybody knows that printing lots of money normally leads to inflation. But how does that work, exactly? Answering that question is key to understanding why it *doesn't* work under current conditions.

First things first: the Fed doesn't actually print money, although its actions can lead to the Treasury's printing money. What the Fed does, when it chooses, is buy assets—normally Treasury bills, aka short-term U.S. government debt, but lately a much wider range of stuff. It also makes direct loans to banks, but that's effectively the same thing; think of it as buying those loans. The crucial thing is where the Fed gets the funds with which it purchases assets. And the answer is that it creates them out of thin air. The Fed approaches, say, Citibank and makes an offer to buy $1 billion worth of Treasury bills. When Citi accepts the offer, it transfers ownership of the bills to the Fed, and in return the Fed credits Citi with $1 billion in the reserve account Citi, like all commercial banks, maintains at the Fed. (Banks can use these reserve accounts much as the rest of us use bank accounts: they can write checks, and they can also withdraw funds in cash if that's what their customers want.) And there's nothing behind that credit; the Fed has the unique right to conjure money into existence whenever it chooses.

What happens next? In normal times Citi doesn't want to leave its funds idle in a reserve account, earning little or no interest, so it withdraws the funds and lends them out. Most of the lent funds end up back at Citi or some other bank—most, but not all, because the public likes to hold some of its wealth in the form of currency, that is, pieces of paper bearing portraits of dead presidents. The funds that do come back to banks can in turn be lent out, and so on.

Even so, how does this translate into inflation? Not directly. The blogger Karl Smith has coined a useful term, "immaculate inflation," by which he means the belief that printing money somehow drives up prices in a way that bypasses the normal forces of supply and demand. That's not how it works. Businesses don't decide to raise their prices because the money supply has gone up; they raise prices because demand for their products has gone up, and they believe that they can mark up their prices without losing too many sales. Workers don't ask for bigger paychecks because they've read about credit expansion; they look for higher wages because jobs have become more available, and their bargaining power has therefore increased. The reason "printing money"—actually, the Fed's purchase of assets with funds created by fiat, but close enough—can lead to inflation is that the credit expansion these Fed purchases set in motion leads to higher spending and higher demand.

And this tells you immediately that the way money-printing causes inflation runs through a boom that causes the economy to overheat. No boom, no inflation; if the economy stays depressed, don't worry about the inflationary consequences of money creation.

What about stagflation, the infamous condition in which inflation is combined with high unemployment? Yes, that sometimes happens. "Supply shocks"—things like harvest failures or oil embargoes—can cause prices of raw materials to rise even though the broader economy is depressed. And these price increases can turn into a more general inflation if lots of workers have pay contracts that are indexed to the cost of living, as was the case in the 1970s, the decade of stagflation. But the twenty-first-century U.S. economy doesn't have many such contracts, and we have in fact had several oil price shocks, most notably in 2007–08, that raised headline consumer prices but never filtered through into wages and hence never caused a wage-price spiral.

Still, you could imagine that all those asset purchases by the Fed could have led to a runaway boom, and hence to an outbreak of inflation. But that obviously didn't happen. Why not?

The answer is that we're in a liquidity trap, with the economy depressed even though short-term interest rates are near zero. What this does is short-circuit the process by which Fed purchases normally lead to a boom and, perhaps, inflation.

Think about what I just said regarding the chain of events started when the Fed buys a bunch of bonds from banks, paying for the bonds by crediting the banks' reserve accounts. In normal times the banks don't want to let the funds sit there; they want to lend them out. But these aren't normal times. Safe assets yield basically zero, which means that safe loans yield almost nothing—so why make them? Unsafe loans, say, to small businesses or corporations with somewhat risky prospects, carry higher interest rates—but they're, well, not safe.

So when the Fed buys assets by crediting banks' reserve accounts, the banks by and large just let the funds sit there. The figure on page 156 shows the total value of those bank accounts over time; they went from trivial to huge after the fall of Lehman Brothers, which is another way of saying that the Fed "printed" a lot of money that didn't actually go anywhere.

Now, it's probably worth saying that this didn't make the Fed's asset purchases pointless. In the months after the fall of Lehman, the Fed made big loans to banks and other financial institutions that probably helped head off an even bigger bank run than we actually had. Then the Fed stepped into the mar-

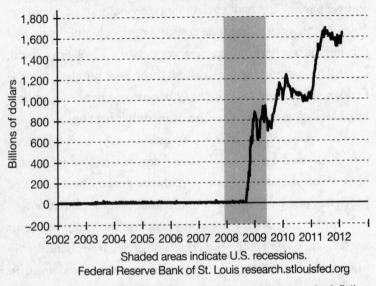

Reserve Balances with Federal Reserve Banks

Shaded areas indicate U.S. recessions.
Federal Reserve Bank of St. Louis research.stlouisfed.org

Bank reserves have soared since the Fed stepped in, but without causing inflation.

Source: Board of Governors of the Federal Reserve System

ket for commercial paper, which businesses use for short-term funding, helping to keep the wheels of commerce turning at a time when banks probably wouldn't have provided the necessary finance. So the Fed was doing things that arguably prevented a much worse financial crisis. It wasn't, however, doing things that would spark off inflation.

But wait, cry some readers—we *are* having lots of inflation. Are we? Let's talk about what the numbers say.

How High Is Inflation, Anyway?

How do we measure inflation? The first port of call is, as it should be, the Consumer Price Index, in which the Bureau of Labor Statistics calculates the cost of a basket of goods and services that is supposed to represent the purchases of a typical household. What does the CPI tell us?

Well, suppose we start from September 2008, the month in which Lehman fell—and, not coincidentally, the month when the Fed began large-scale asset purchases, "printing money" on a massive scale. Over the course of the next three years, consumer prices rose a grand total of 3.6 percent, or 1.2 percent a year. That doesn't sound like the "severe inflation" many were predicting, far less the Zimbabwefication of America.

That said, the rate of inflation wasn't constant through that period. In the first year after the failure of Lehman, prices actually fell 1.3 percent; in the second, they rose 1.1 percent; in the third, they rose 3.9 percent. Was inflation taking off?

Actually, no. By early 2012, inflation was clearly subsiding; average inflation at an annual rate over the previous six months had been only 1.8 percent, and markets seemed to expect inflation to stay low looking forward. And this came as no surprise to many economists, myself (and Ben Bernanke) included. For we had argued all along that the rise in inflation that took place in late 2010 and the first half of 2011 was a temporary blip, reflecting a bulge in world prices of oil and other commodities, and that no real inflationary process was under way, no big rise in underlying inflation in the United States.

But what do I mean by "underlying inflation"? Here we have to talk briefly about a grossly misunderstood concept, the notion of "core" inflation. Why do we need such a concept, and how should it be measured?

Core inflation is usually measured by taking food and energy out of the price index; but there are a number of alternative measures, all of them trying to get at the same thing.

First, let me clear up a couple of misconceptions. Core inflation is *not* used for things like calculating cost-of-living adjustments for Social Security; those use the regular CPI.

And people who say things like "That's a stupid concept—people have to spend money on food and gas, so they should be in your inflation measures" are missing the point. Core inflation isn't supposed to measure the cost of living; it's supposed to measure something else: inflation inertia.

Think about it this way. Some prices in the economy fluctuate all the time in the face of supply and demand; food and fuel are the obvious examples. Many prices, however, don't fluctuate this way; they're set by companies that have only a few competitors, or are negotiated in long-term contracts, so they're revised only at intervals ranging from months to years. Many wages are set the same way.

The key thing about these less flexible prices is that because they aren't revised very often, they're set with future inflation in mind. Suppose that I'm setting my price for the next year, and that I expect the overall level of prices—including things like the average price of competing goods—to rise 10 percent over the course of the year. Then I'm probably going to set my price about 5 percent higher than I would if I were taking only current conditions into account.

And that's not the whole story: because temporarily fixed prices are revised only at intervals, their resets often involve catch-up. Again, suppose that I set my prices once a year, and there's an overall inflation rate of 10 percent. Then at the time I reset my prices, they'll probably be about 5 percent lower than they "should" be; add that effect to the anticipation of future inflation, and I'll probably mark up my price by 10 percent—*even if supply and demand are more or less balanced right now.*

Now imagine an economy in which everyone is doing this. What this tells us is that inflation tends to be self-perpetuating, unless there's a big excess of either supply or demand. In particular, once expectations of, say, persistent 10 percent infla-tion have become "embedded" in the economy, it will take a major period of slack—years of high unemployment—to get that rate down. A case in point is the disinflation of the early 1980s, in which it took a very severe recession to get inflation from around 10 percent down to around 4 percent.

On the other hand, a burst of inflation that isn't embedded in this way can quickly subside, or even go into reverse. In 2007–08 there was a surge in oil and food prices, driven by a combination of bad weather and rising demand from emerg-ing economies like China's, that sent inflation as measured by the CPI briefly soaring to 5.5 percent—but commodity prices then proceeded to plunge again, and inflation went negative.

How you should react to rising inflation therefore depends on whether it's something like the price rise of 2007–08, a temporary blip, or whether it's the kind of inflation increase that seems to be getting embedded in the economy and will be hard to undo.

And if you were paying close attention in the period from the fall of 2010 to the summer of 2011, what you saw was something that looked broadly similar to 2007–08. Oil and other commodity prices went way up over a roughly six-month period, again largely thanks to demand from China and other emerging economies, but price measures that excluded food and energy went up much less, and wage growth didn't accel-erate at all. In June 2011 Ben Bernanke declared that "there is not much evidence that inflation is becoming broad-based or ingrained in our economy; indeed, increases in the price of a single product—gasoline—account for the bulk of the recent increase in consumer price inflation," and he went on to pre-dict that inflation would subside in the months ahead.

He was, of course, pilloried by many on the right for his nonchalance about inflation. Nearly everyone on the Republican side of the political divide saw the rise in commodity prices not as a temporary factor distorting headline inflation numbers but as the leading edge of a great inflationary surge, and anyone who begged to differ could expect a vitriolic response. But Bernanke was right: the rise in inflation was indeed temporary, and has already gone away.

But can you trust the numbers? Let me make one more digression, into the world of inflation conspiracy theories.

Faced with the consistent failure of inflation to take off the way it was supposed to, inflation worriers have several choices. They can admit that they were wrong; they can just ignore the data; or they can claim that the data lie, that the feds are hiding the true rate of inflation. Very few, as far as I can tell, have chosen option 1; my experience in a decade of punditry is that almost nobody ever admits to having been wrong about anything. Many have chosen option 2, simply ignoring the wrongness of their past predictions. But a significant number have taken refuge in option 3, buying into claims that the Bureau of Labor Statistics (BLS) is massaging the data to hide actual inflation. These claims received fairly high-profile support when Niall Ferguson, the historian and commentator I mentioned in the discussion of deficits and their impact, used his *Newsweek* column to endorse claims that inflation is actually running at around 10 percent.

How do we know that this is wrong? Well, you can look at what the BLS actually does—it's quite transparent—and see that it's reasonable. Or you can notice that if inflation were really running at 10 percent, workers' purchasing power would be plummeting, which isn't consistent with what observation tells us—stagnating, yes, but plummeting, no. Best of all, however, you can just compare the official price statistics with independently generated private estimates, most notably the Internet-based estimates of MIT's Billion Prices Project. And these private estimates basically match the official numbers.

Of course, maybe MIT is also part of the conspiracy . . .

In the end, then, all that inflation fearmongering has been about a nonexistent threat. Underlying inflation is low and, given the depressed state of the economy, likely to go even lower in the years ahead.

And that's not a good thing. Falling inflation, and even worse, possible deflation, will make recovery from this depression much harder. What we should be aiming for is the opposite: moderately higher inflation, say core inflation of around 4 percent. (This was, by the way, the rate that prevailed during Ronald Reagan's second term.)

The Case for Higher Inflation

In February 2010 the International Monetary Fund released a paper written by Olivier Blanchard, its chief economist, and two of his colleagues, under the innocuous-sounding title "Rethinking Macroeconomic Policy." The contents of the paper, however, weren't quite what you'd expect to hear from the IMF. It was an exercise in soul-searching, questioning the assumptions on which the IMF and almost everyone else in responsible positions had based policy for the past twenty years. Most notably, it suggested that central banks like the Fed and the European Central Bank might have aimed for excessively low inflation, that it might be better to aim for 4 percent inflation rather than the 2 percent or less that has become the norm for "sound" policy.

Many of us were surprised—not so much by the fact that Blanchard, a very eminent macroeconomist, *thinks* such things, but by the fact that he was allowed to say them. Blanchard was a colleague of mine at MIT for many years, and his views about how the economy works are, I believe, not too different from mine. It speaks well for the IMF, however, that it let such views receive a public airing, if not exactly an institutional imprimatur.

But what is the case for higher inflation? As we'll see in a minute, there are actually three reasons why higher inflation would be helpful, given the situation we're in. Before I get there, however, let's ask about the costs of inflation. How bad a thing would it be if prices were rising 4 percent a year instead of 2 percent?

The answer, according to most economists who have tried to put a number to it, is that the costs would be minor. Very high inflation can impose large economic costs, both because it discourages the use of money—pushing people back toward a barter economy—and because it makes planning very difficult. Nobody wants to minimize the horrors of a Weimar type of situation in which people use lumps of coal for money, and in which both long-term contracts and informative accounting become impossible.

But 4 percent inflation doesn't produce even a ghost of these effects. Again, the inflation rate was about 4 percent during Reagan's second term, and that didn't seem especially disruptive at the time.

Meanwhile, a somewhat higher inflation rate could have three benefits.

The first, which is the one Blanchard and colleagues emphasized, is that a higher normal inflation rate could loosen the constraints imposed by the fact that interest rates can't go below zero. Irving Fisher—the same Irving Fisher who came up with the concept of debt deflation, the key to understanding the depression we're in—pointed out long ago that higher expected inflation, other things being equal, makes borrowing more attractive: if borrowers believe that they'll be able to repay loans in dollars that are worth less than the dollars they borrow today, they'll be more willing to borrow and spend at any given interest rate.

In normal times this increased willingness to borrow is canceled out by higher interest rates: in theory, and to a large extent in practice, higher expected inflation is matched one-for-one by higher rates. But right now we're in a liquidity trap, in which interest rates in a sense "want" to go below zero but can't, because people have the option of just holding cash. In this situation, higher expected inflation would not, at least at first, translate into higher interest rates, so it would in fact lead to more borrowing.

Or to put it a bit differently (and the way Blanchard actually put it), if inflation had generally been around 4 instead of 2 percent before the crisis, short-term interest rates would have been around 7 percent instead of around 5, and the Fed would therefore have had that much more room to cut when crisis struck.

Yet that isn't the only reason higher inflation would be helpful. There's also the debt overhang—the excessive private debt that set the stage for the Minsky moment and the slump that followed. Deflation, said Fisher, can depress the economy by raising the real value of debt. Inflation, conversely, can help by reducing that real value. Right now, markets seem to expect the U.S. price level to be around 8 percent higher in 2017 than it is today. If we could manage 4 or 5 percent inflation over that stretch, so that prices were 25 percent higher, the real value of mortgage debt would be substantially lower than it looks on current prospect—and the economy would therefore be substantially farther along the road to sustained recovery.

There's one more argument for higher inflation, which isn't particularly important for the United States but is very important for Europe: wages are subject to "downward nominal rigidity," which is econospeak for the fact, overwhelmingly borne out by recent experience, that workers are very unwilling to accept explicit pay cuts. If you say, but of course they are, you're missing the point: workers are much less willing to accept, say, a 5 percent cut in the number on their paycheck than they are to accept an unchanged paycheck whose purchasing power is eroded by inflation. Nor should we declare that workers are stubborn or stupid here: it's very difficult when you are asked to take a pay cut to know whether you're being taken advantage of by your employer, whereas the question doesn't arise when forces that are clearly not under your boss's control raise your cost of living.

This downward nominal rigidity—sorry, sometimes jargon really is needed to specify a particular concept—is probably the reason we haven't seen actual deflation in the United States, despite the depressed economy. Some workers are still getting raises, for a variety of reasons; relatively few are seeing their pay actually fall. So the overall level of wages is still rising slowly despite mass unemployment, which in turn is helping keep overall prices rising slowly too.

This is not a problem for America. On the contrary, the last thing we need right now is a general fall in wages, exacerbating the problem of debt deflation. But as we'll see in the next chapter, it is a big problem for some European nations, which badly need to cut their wages relative to wages in Germany. It's a terrible problem, but one that would be made considerably less terrible if Europe had 3 or 4 percent inflation, not the slightly more than 1 percent that markets expect to prevail in coming years. More on all that, coming next.

Now, you may wonder what good it is wishing for higher inflation. Remember, the doctrine of immaculate inflation is nonsense: no boom, no inflation. And how can we get a boom?

The answer is that we need a combination of strong fiscal stimulus and supportive policies by the Fed and its counterparts abroad. But we'll get there later in this book.

Let's sum up where we are now. For the past several years, we have been subjected to a series of dire warnings about the dangers of inflation. Yet it was clear, to those who understood the nature of the depression we're in, that these warnings were all wrong; and sure enough, the great inflation surge keeps not happening. The reality is that inflation is actually too low, and in Europe, where we go next, that is part of an extremely dire situation.

CHAPTER TEN

EURODÄMMERUNG

It is now ten years since a pioneering group of EU Member States took a momentous step and launched the single currency, the euro. After many years of careful preparations, on 1 January 1999 the euro became the official currency for over 300 million citizens in the newly created euro area. And three years later, on New Year's Day 2002, shiny new euro coins and crisp new euro banknotes began to appear, replacing 12 national currencies in people's purses and pockets. A decade into its existence, we are celebrating economic and monetary union and the euro, and looking at how it has fulfilled its promise.

There have been welcome changes since the euro was launched: today, the euro area has grown to 15 countries with the arrival of Slovenia in 2007 and Cyprus and Malta in 2008. And employment and growth are rising as economic performance improves. Furthermore, the euro is progressively becoming a truly international currency and giving the euro area a bigger voice in international economic affairs.

Yet the benefits that the euro has brought are not only found in numbers and statistics. It has also introduced more choice, more certainty, more security and more opportunities in citizens' everyday lives. In this brochure, we present some examples of how the euro has achieved, and continues to achieve, real improvements on the ground for people across Europe.*

—Introduction to "Ten Years of the Euro:
10 Success Stories," a brochure released by
the European Commission at the beginning of 2009

FOR THE PAST few years the comparison between economic developments in Europe and in the United States has seemed like a race between the halt and the lame—or, if you like, a

---

*The people featured in these ten success stories are fictional: they describe typical situations based on real data.

competition over who can bungle the crisis response more. At the time of writing, Europe seemed to be nosing ahead in the race to disaster, but give it time.

If this seems hard-hearted, or sounds like American gloating, let me be clear: the economic travails of Europe are a truly terrible thing, not just because of the pain they inflict but also because of their political implications. For some sixty years Europe has been engaged in a noble experiment, an attempt to reform a war-torn continent with economic integration, setting it permanently on the path of peace and democracy. The whole world has a stake in the success of that experiment, and will suffer if it fails.

The experiment began in 1951, with the creation of the European Coal and Steel Community. Don't let the prosaic name fool you: this was a highly idealistic attempt to make war within Europe impossible. By establishing free trade in, well, coal and steel—that is, by eliminating all tariffs and all restrictions on cross-border economic shipments, so that steel mills could buy coal from the closest producer, even if it was on the other side of the border—the pact produced economic gains. But it also ensured that French steel mills relied on German coal and vice versa, so that any future hostilities between the nations would be extremely disruptive and, it was hoped, unthinkable.

The Coal and Steel Community was a great success, and it set the model for a series of similar moves. In 1957 six European nations established the European Economic Community, a customs union with free trade among its members and common tariffs on imports from outside. In the 1970s Britain, Ireland, and Denmark joined the group; meanwhile, the European Community expanded its role, becoming a provider of aid to poorer regions and promoting democratic governments throughout Europe. In the 1980s, Spain, Portugal, and Greece, having gotten rid of their dictators, were rewarded with membership in the community—and European nations moved to deepen their economic ties by harmonizing economic regulations, removing border posts, and guaranteeing free movement of workers.

At each stage, economic gains from closer integration were paired with an ever-closer degree of political integration. Economic policies were never just about the economics; they were always also about promoting European unity. For example, the economic case for free trade between Spain and France was just as good when Generalissimo Francisco Franco still ruled as it was after his death (and the problems with Spanish entry were just as real after his death as before), but adding a democratic Spain to the European project was a worthwhile goal in a way that free trade with a dictatorship wouldn't have been. And this helps explain what now looks like a fateful error— the decision to move to a common currency: European elites were so enthralled with the idea of creating a powerful symbol of unity that they played up the gains from a single currency and brushed aside warnings of a significant downside.

The Trouble with (One) Money

There are, of course, real costs to the use of multiple currencies, costs that can be avoided by the adoption of a common currency. Cross-border business is more expensive if currencies must be exchanged, multiple currencies kept on hand, and/or bank accounts in multiple currencies maintained. The possibility of exchange rate fluctuations introduces uncertainty; planning becomes more difficult and accounting less clear when income and expenses aren't always in the same units. The more business a political unit does with its neighbors, the more problematic it would be to have an independent currency, which is why it wouldn't be a good idea for, say, Brooklyn to have its own dollar the way Canada does.

But there are also significant advantages to having your own currency, of which the best understood is the way that devaluation—reducing the value of your currency in terms of other currencies—can sometimes ease the process of adjusting to an economic shock.

Consider this not at all hypothetical example: Suppose that Spain has spent much of the past decade buoyed by a huge housing boom, financed by large inflows of capital from Germany. This boom has fueled inflation and pushed Spanish wages up relative to wages in Germany. But the boom turns out to have been inflated by a bubble and has now gone bust. As a result, Spain needs to reorient its economy away from construction and back toward manufacturing. But at this point Spanish manufacturing isn't competitive, because Spanish wages are too high compared with German wages. How can Spain become competitive again?

One way to get there is to persuade or push Spanish workers into accepting lower wages. That is in fact the only way to get there if Spain and Germany have the same currency, or if Spain's currency is, as a matter of unalterable policy, fixed against Germany's currency.

But if Spain has its own currency, and is willing to let it fall, its wages can be brought in line simply by devaluing that currency. Go from 80 pesetas per Deutsche mark to 100 pesetas per Deutsche mark, while keeping Spanish wages *in pesetas* unchanged, and at a stroke you've reduced Spanish wages relative to German wages by 20 percent.

Why is this any easier than just negotiating lower wages? The best explanation comes from none other than Milton Friedman, who made the case for flexible exchange rates in a classic 1953 article, "The Case for Flexible Exchange Rates," in *Essays in Positive Economics*. Here's what he wrote:

> The argument for flexible exchange rates is, strange to say, very nearly identical with the argument for daylight saving time. Isn't it absurd to change the clock in summer when exactly the same result could be achieved by having each individual change his habits? All that is required is that everyone decide to come to his office an hour earlier, have lunch an hour earlier, etc. But obviously it is much simpler to change the clock that guides all than to have each individual separately change his pattern of reaction to the clock, even though all want to do so. The situation is exactly the same in the exchange market. It is far simpler to allow one price to change, namely, the price of foreign exchange, than to rely upon changes in the multitude of prices that together constitute the internal price structure.

That's clearly right. Workers are always reluctant to accept wage cuts, but they're especially reluctant if they aren't sure whether other workers will accept similar cuts and whether the cost of living will be falling as labor costs fall. No country that I'm aware of has the kind of labor market and institutions that would make it easy to respond to the situation I've just described for Spain by means of across-the-board wage cuts. But countries can and do get large declines in their relative wages more or less overnight, and with very little disruption, by means of currency devaluation.

So establishing a common currency involves a trade-off.

On one side, there are efficiency gains from sharing a currency: business costs decline, business planning presumably improves. On the other side, there is a loss of flexibility, which can be a big problem if there are large "asymmetric shocks" like the collapse of a housing boom in some but not all countries.

It's hard to put a number to the value of economic flexibility. It's even harder to put a number to the gains from a shared currency. There is, nonetheless, an extensive economics literature on the criteria for an "optimum currency area," the ugly but useful term of art for a group of countries that would gain from merging their currencies. What does this literature say?

First, it doesn't make sense for countries to share a currency unless they do a lot of business with one another. Back in the 1990s Argentina fixed the value of the peso at one U.S. dollar, supposedly forever, which wasn't quite the same thing as giving up its currency but was intended to be the next best thing. As it turned out, however, it was a doomed venture that eventually ended with devaluation and default. One reason it was doomed was that Argentina isn't all that closely linked, economically, with the United States, which accounts for only 11 percent of its imports and 5 percent of its exports. On one side, whatever gains there were from giving businesses certainty about the dollar–peso rate were fairly small, since Argentina did so little trade with the United States. On the other side, Argentina was whipsawed by fluctuations in other currencies, notably big falls in both the euro and Brazil's real against the dollar, which left Argentina's exports seriously overpriced.

On this score, Europe looked good: European nations do about 60 percent of their trade with one another, and they do a *lot* of trade. On two other important criteria, however—labor mobility and fiscal integration—Europe didn't look nearly as well suited for a single currency.

Labor mobility took center stage in the paper that started the whole optimum currency area field, written by the Canadian-born economist Robert Mundell in 1961. A rough synopsis of Mundell's argument would be that the problems of adjusting to a simultaneous boom in Saskatchewan and slump in British Columbia, or vice versa, are substantially less if workers move freely to wherever the jobs are. And labor does in fact move freely among Canadian provinces, Quebec excepted; it moves freely among U.S. states. It does not, however, move freely among European nations. Even though Europeans have since 1992 had the legal right to take work anywhere in the European Union, linguistic and cultural divisions are large enough that even large differences in unemployment lead to only modest amounts of migration.

The importance of fiscal integration was highlighted by Princeton's Peter Kenen a few years after Mundell's paper. To illustrate Kenen's point, consider a comparison between two economies that, scenery aside, look quite similar at the moment: Ireland and Nevada. Both had huge housing bubbles that have burst; both were plunged into deep recessions that sent unemployment soaring; in both there have been many defaults on home mortgages.

But in the case of Nevada, these shocks are buffered, to an important extent, by the federal government. Nevada is paying a lot less in taxes to Washington these days, but the state's older residents are still getting their Social Security checks, and Medicare is still paying their medical bills—so in effect the state is receiving a great deal of aid. Meanwhile, deposits in Nevada's banks are guaranteed by a federal agency, the FDIC, and some of the losses from mortgage defaults are falling on Fannie and Freddie, which are backed by the federal government.

Ireland, by contrast, is mostly on its own, having to bail out its own banks, having to pay for retirement and health care out of its own greatly diminished revenue. So although times are tough in both places, Ireland is in crisis in a way that Nevada isn't.

And none of this comes as a surprise. Twenty years ago, as the idea of a common European currency began moving toward reality, the problematic case for creating that currency was widely understood. There was, in fact, an extensive academic discussion of the issue (in which I was a participant), and the American economists involved were, in general, skeptical of the case for the euro—mainly because the United States seemed to offer a good model of what it takes to make an economy suitable for a single currency, and Europe fell far short of that model. Labor mobility, we thought, was just too weak, and the lack of a central government and the automatic buffering such a government would provide added to the doubts.

But these warnings were brushed aside. The glamour, if you can call it that, of the euro idea, the sense that Europe was taking a momentous step forward toward finally ending its history of war and becoming a beacon of democracy, was just too strong. When one asked how Europe would handle situations in which some economies were doing well while others were slumping—as is the case for Germany and Spain, respectively, right now—the official answer, more or less, was that all the nations of the euro area would follow sound policies, so that there would be no such "asymmetric shocks," and if they did somehow happen, "structural reform" would render European economies flexible enough to make the necessary adjustments.

What actually happened, however, was the mother of all asymmetric shocks. And it was the creation of the euro itself that caused it.

The Eurobubble

The euro officially came into existence at the beginning of 1999, although euro notes and coins didn't arrive for another three years. (Officially, the franc, the mark, the lira, and so on became denominations of the euro, with 1 French franc = 1/6.5597th of a euro, 1 Deutsche mark = 1/1.95583th of a euro, and so on.) It immediately had a fateful effect: it made investors feel safe.

More specifically, it made investors feel safe putting their money into countries that had previously been considered risky. Interest rates in southern Europe had historically been substantially higher than rates in Germany, because investors demanded a premium to compensate for the risk of devaluation and/or default. With the coming of the euro, those premiums collapsed: Spanish debt, Italian debt, and even Greek debt were treated as being almost as safe as German debt.

This amounted to a big cut in the cost of borrowed money in southern Europe; it led to huge housing booms that quickly turned into huge housing bubbles.

The mechanics of these housing booms/bubbles were somewhat different from the mechanics of the U.S. bubble: there was much less fancy finance, more straight lending by conventional banks. Local banks, however, didn't have nearly enough deposits to support all the lending they were doing, so they turned on a massive scale to the wholesale market, borrowing funds from banks in the European "core"—mainly Germany—which wasn't experiencing a comparable boom. So there were massive flows of capital from Europe's core to its booming periphery.

These inflows of capital fed booms that in turn led to rising wages: in the decade after the euro's creation, unit labor costs (wages adjusted for productivity) rose about 35 percent in southern Europe, compared with a rise of only 9 percent in Germany. Manufacturing in Europe's south became uncompetitive, which in turn meant that the countries that were attracting huge money inflows began running correspondingly huge trade deficits. Just to give you a sense of what was happening—and what now has to be unwound—the figure below shows the rise of trade imbalances within Europe after the introduction of the euro. One line shows Germany's current account balance (a broad measure of the trade balance); the other shows the combined current account balances of the GIPSI countries (Greece, Ireland, Portugal, Spain, Italy). That widening spread is at the heart of Europe's problems.

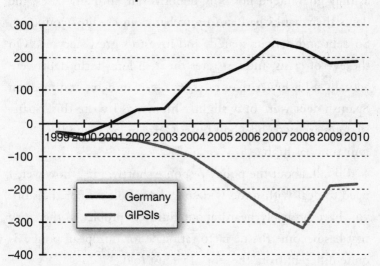

European Trade Imbalances

After the creation of the euro, the GIPSI economies (Greece, Ireland, Portugal, Spain, Italy) moved into huge deficits in their current accounts, a broad measure of the trade balance. Meanwhile, Germany moved into a huge matching surplus.

Source: International Monetary Fund

But few realized how great the danger was as it was building. Instead, there was complacency bordering on euphoria. Then the bubbles burst.

The financial crisis in the United States triggered the collapse in Europe, but the collapse would have happened sooner or later in any case. And suddenly the euro found itself facing a huge asymmetrical shock, one that was made much worse by the absence of fiscal integration.

For the bursting of those housing bubbles, which happened a bit later than in the United States but was well under way by 2008, did more than plunge the bubble countries into recession: it put their budgets under severe strain. Revenues plunged along with output and employment; spending on unemployment benefits soared; and governments found (or placed) themselves on the hook for expensive bank bailouts, as they guaranteed not only deposits but, in many cases, the debts their banks had run up to banks in creditor countries. So debt and deficits soared, and investors grew nervous. On the eve of crisis, interest rates on Irish long-term debt were actually a bit lower than rates on German debt, and rates on Spanish debt were only slightly higher; as I write this, Spanish rates are two and a half times German rates, and Irish rates four times as high.

I'll talk about the policy response shortly. First, however, I need to deal with some widespread mythology. For the story you have probably heard about Europe's problems, the story that has become the de facto rationale for European policy, is quite different from the story I've just told.

Europe's Big Delusion

In chapter 4 I described and debunked the Big Lie about America's crisis, the claim that government agencies caused a crisis by mistakenly trying to help the poor. Well, Europe has its own distorting narrative, a false account of the causes of crisis that gets in the way of real solutions and in fact leads to policies that make things worse.

I don't think the purveyors of the false European narrative are as cynical as their American counterparts; I don't see as much deliberate cooking of the data, and I suspect most of them believe what they are saying. So let's call it a Big Delusion rather than a Big Lie. Yet it's not clear that this makes it any better; it's still dead wrong, and the people propounding this doctrine are just as unwilling as the U.S. right to listen to contrary evidence.

So here's Europe's Big Delusion: it's the belief that Europe's crisis was essentially caused by fiscal irresponsibility. Countries ran excessive budget deficits, the story goes, getting themselves too deep into debt—and the important thing now is to impose rules that will keep this from ever happening again.

But, some readers are surely asking, isn't this pretty much what happened in Greece? And the answer is yes, although even the Greek story is more complicated than that. The point, however, is that it's not what happened in the other crisis countries—and if this were only a Greek problem, it would not be the crisis it is. For Greece has a small economy, accounting for less than 3 percent of the combined GDP of the euro nations and only about 8 percent of the combined GDP of the euro nations in crisis.

How misleading is the "Hellenization" of discourse in

Europe? One can, maybe, make a case for fiscal irresponsibility in Portugal, too, although not on the same scale. But Ireland had a budget surplus and low debt on the eve of crisis; in 2006 George Osborne, now running Britain's economic policy, called it "a shining example of the art of the possible in long-term economic policy-making." Spain also had a budget surplus and low debt. Italy had a high level of debt inherited from the 1970s and 1980s, when policy really was irresponsible, but was steadily bringing the ratio of debt to GDP down.

GIPSI Debt/GDP

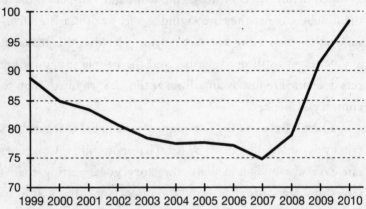

As a group, the European nations now in fiscal trouble were steadily improving their debt position until the financial crisis struck.

Source: International Monetary Fund

How did all this add up? The figure above shows debt as a percentage of GDP for the "average" country now in crisis—an average, weighted by GDP, of the debt-to-GDP ratios for the five GIPSI countries (again, Greece, Ireland, Portugal, Spain, Italy). Up through 2007 this average was steadily declining—that is, far from looking as if they were being profligate, the GIPSIs as a group seemed to be improving their fiscal position over time. It was only with the crisis that debt soared.

Yet many Europeans in key positions—especially politicians and officials in Germany, but also the leadership of the European Central Bank and opinion leaders throughout the world of finance and banking—are deeply committed to the Big Delusion, and no amount of contrary evidence will shake them. As a result, the problem of dealing with the crisis is often couched in moral terms: nations are in trouble because they have sinned, and they must redeem themselves through suffering.

And that's a very bad way to approach the actual problems Europe faces.

Europe's Essential Problem

If you look at Europe, or more specifically the euro area, in aggregate—that is, add up the numbers from all of the countries using the euro—it doesn't look as if it should be in such bad shape. Both private and public debt are somewhat lower than in the United States, suggesting that there should be more room for maneuver; inflation numbers look similar to ours, with no hint of an inflationary outbreak; and, for what it's worth, Europe as a whole has a roughly balanced current account, meaning that it has no need to attract capital from elsewhere.

But Europe is not an aggregate. It's a collection of nations that have their own budgets (because there's very little fiscal integration) and their own labor markets (because labor mobility is low)—but that don't have their own currencies. And that creates a crisis.

Think about Spain, which I consider the emblematic euro crisis economy—and ignore, for a moment, the question of the government budget. As we've already seen, during the first eight years of the euro, Spain experienced huge inflows of money that fed a massive housing bubble, and also led to a large rise in wages and prices relative to those in the core European economies. The essential Spanish problem, from which all else flows, is the need to get its costs and prices back in line. How can that happen?

Well, it could happen through inflation in the core economies. Suppose that the European Central Bank (ECB) followed an easy-money policy while the German government engaged in fiscal stimulus; this would mean full employment in Germany even as high unemployment persisted in Spain. So Spanish wages wouldn't rise much if at all, while German wages would rise a lot; Spanish costs would therefore hold level while German costs rose. And that would be a relatively easy adjustment on Spain's part—not easy, just *relatively* easy.

But the Germans hate, hate, hate the idea of inflation, thanks to memories of the great inflation of the early 1920s. (Curiously, there is much less memory of the deflationary policies of the early 1930s, which are what actually set the stage for the rise of you-know-who. More in chapter 11.) And perhaps more directly relevant, the ECB's mandate calls on it to maintain price stability—period. It's an open question how binding that mandate really is, and I suspect that the ECB could find a way to rationalize moderate inflation despite what the charter says. But the mind-set is certainly one in which inflation is considered a great evil, no matter what the consequences of a low-inflation policy may be.

Now think about what this implies for Spain—namely, that it has to get its costs in line through deflation, what is known in eurojargon as "internal devaluation." And that's a very hard thing to achieve, because wages are downwardly rigid: they fall only slowly and grudgingly, even in the face of massive unemployment.

If there were any doubts about that downward rigidity, the track record in Europe should dispel them. Consider the case of Ireland, generally thought of as a nation with highly "flexible" labor markets—another euphemism, meaning an economy in which employers can relatively easily fire workers and/or cut their paychecks. Despite several years of incredibly high unemployment (around 14 percent at the time of writing), Irish wages have fallen only about 4 percent from their peak. So yes, Ireland is achieving internal devaluation, but very slowly. The story is similar in Latvia, which isn't on the euro but has rejected the notion of devaluing its currency. In Spain itself, average wages have actually risen slightly despite very high unemployment, although this may be partly a statistical illusion.

By the way, if you want an illustration of Milton Friedman's point that it's much easier to cut wages and prices by simply devaluing your currency, look at Iceland. The tiny island nation is famous for the scale of its financial disaster, and you might have expected it to be doing even worse right now than Ireland. But Iceland declared that it had no responsibility for the debts of its runaway bankers, and it also enjoyed the great advantage of still having its own currency, which made it very easy to regain competitiveness: it simply let the krona fall, and just like that its wages in terms of the euro were cut 25 percent.

Spain, however, doesn't have its own currency. This means that to get their costs in line, Spain and other countries will have to go through an extended period of very high unemployment, high enough to slowly grind wages down. And that's not all. The countries that are now being forced to get their costs in line are also the countries that had the biggest buildup of private debt before the crisis. Now they're faced with deflation, which will increase the real burden of that debt.

But what about the fiscal crisis, the soaring interest rates on government debt in southern Europe? To a large extent, this fiscal crisis is a byproduct of the problem of burst bubbles and out-of-line costs. When the crisis struck, deficits soared, while debt took a sudden leap upward as the troubled countries moved to bail out their banking systems. And the usual way governments end up dealing with high debt burdens— a combination of inflation and growth, which erodes debt relative to GDP—isn't a path available to euro area nations, which are instead condemned to years of deflation and stagnation. No surprise, then, that investors wonder whether the nations of southern Europe will be willing or able to pay their debts in full.

Yet that's not the whole story. There's another element in the euro crisis, another weakness of a shared currency, that took many people, myself included, by surprise. It turns out that countries that lack their own currency are highly vulnerable to self-fulfilling panic, in which the efforts of investors to avoid losses from default end up triggering the very default they fear.

This point was first made by the Belgian economist Paul De Grauwe, who noted that interest rates on British debt are much lower than rates on Spanish debt—2 percent and 5 percent, respectively, at the time of writing—even though Britain has higher debt and deficits, and arguably a worse fiscal outlook than Spain, even taking into account Spain's deflation.

But as De Grauwe pointed out, Spain faces one risk Britain doesn't: a freeze-up of liquidity.

Here's what he meant. Just about every modern government has a fair bit of debt, and it's not all thirty-year bonds; there's a lot of very short-term debt with a maturity of only a few months, plus two-, three-, or five-year bonds, many of which come due in any given year. Governments depend on being able to roll over most of this debt, in effect selling new bonds to pay off old ones. If for some reason investors should refuse to buy new bonds, even a basically solvent government could be forced into default.

Could this happen to the United States? Actually, no—because the Federal Reserve could and would step in and buy federal debt, in effect printing money to pay the government's bills. Nor could it happen to Britain, or Japan, or any country that borrows in its own currency and has its own central bank. But it could happen to any of the countries now on the euro, which cannot count on the European Central Bank to provide cash in an emergency. And if a euro area country should be forced into default by this kind of cash squeeze, it might end up never paying its debts in full.

This immediately creates the possibility of a self-fulfilling crisis, in which investors' fears of a default brought on by a cash squeeze lead them to shun a country's bonds, bringing on the very cash squeeze they fear. And even if such a crisis hasn't happened yet, it's easy to see how ongoing nervousness about the possibility of such crises can lead investors to demand higher interest rates in order to hold debt of countries potentially subject to self-fulfilling panic.

Sure enough, since early 2011 there has been a clear euro penalty, in which countries that use the euro face higher costs of borrowing than countries with similar economic and fiscal outlooks that retain their own currencies. It's not just Spain versus the United Kingdom; my favorite comparison is among three Scandinavian countries, Finland, Sweden, and Denmark, all of which should be considered highly creditworthy. Yet Finland, which is on the euro, has seen its borrowing costs rise substantially above those of Sweden, which has kept its own, freely floating currency, and even those of Denmark, which maintains a fixed exchange rate against the euro but retains its own currency and hence the potential to bail itself out in a cash squeeze.

Saving the Euro

Given the troubles the euro is now experiencing, it looks as if the euroskeptics, who warned that Europe wasn't really suited for a single currency, were right. Furthermore, those countries that chose not to adopt the euro—Britain, Sweden—are having a much easier time than their euro-using neighbors. So should European countries now in trouble simply reverse course and return to independent currencies?

Not necessarily. Even euroskeptics like me realize that breaking up the euro now that it exists would have very serious costs. For one thing, any country that seemed likely to exit the euro would immediately face a huge run on its banks, as depositors raced to move their funds to more solid euro nations. And the return of the drachma or the peseta would create huge legal problems, as everyone tried to figure out the meaning of debts and contracts denominated in euros.

Moreover, an about-face on the euro would be a dramatic political defeat for the broader European project of unity and democracy through economic integration—a project that, as

I said at the beginning, is very important not just for Europe but for the world.

So it would be best if a way could be found to save the euro. How might that be accomplished?

First, and most urgently, Europe needs to put a stop to panic attacks. One way or another, there has to be a guarantee of adequate liquidity—a guarantee that governments won't simply run out of cash because of market panic—comparable to the guarantee that exists in practice for governments that borrow in their own currency. The most obvious way to do this would be for the European Central Bank to stand ready to buy government bonds of euro nations.

Second, those nations whose costs and prices are way out of line—the European countries that have been running large trade deficits, but can't continue to do so—need a plausible path back to being competitive. In the short run, surplus countries have to be a source of strong demand for deficit countries' exports. And over time, if this path isn't going to involve extremely costly deflation in the deficit countries, it will have to involve moderate but significant inflation in the surplus countries, and a somewhat lower but still significant inflation rate—say, 3 or 4 percent—for the euro area as a whole. What this adds up to is very expansionary monetary policy from the ECB plus fiscal stimulus in Germany and a few smaller countries.

Finally, although fiscal issues aren't at the heart of the problem, the deficit countries do at this point have debt and deficit problems, and will have to practice considerable fiscal austerity over time to put their fiscal houses in order.

So that's what it would probably take to save the euro. Is anything like this in the cards?

The ECB has surprised on the upside since Mario Draghi took over from Jean-Claude Trichet as president. True, Draghi firmly turned away demands that he buy the bonds of crisis countries. But he found a way to achieve more or less the same result through the back door, announcing a program in which the ECB would advance unlimited loans to private banks, accepting the bonds of European governments as collateral. The result is that prospects of a self-fulfilling panic leading to stratospheric interest rates on European bonds have at the time of writing receded.

Even with this, however, the most extreme cases—Greece, Portugal, and Ireland—remain shut out of private capital markets. So they've been reliant on a series of ad hoc lending programs from the "troika" of stronger European governments, the ECB, and the International Monetary Fund. Unfortunately, the troika has consistently provided too little money, too late. And in return for this emergency lending, deficit countries have been required to impose immediate, draconian programs of spending cuts and tax hikes—programs that push them into even deeper slumps and that keep falling short even in purely budgetary terms as shrinking economies cause falling tax receipts.

Meanwhile, nothing has been done to provide an environment in which deficit countries have a plausible path to restored competitiveness. Even as deficit countries are pushed into savage austerity, surplus countries have been engaged in austerity programs of their own, undermining hopes for export growth. And far from accepting the need for somewhat higher inflation, the European Central Bank raised interest rates in the first half of 2011 to ward off an inflation threat that existed only in its mind. (The rate hikes were reversed later, but a great deal of damage had been done.)

Why has Europe responded so badly to its crisis? I've already suggested part of the answer: much of the continent's leadership seems determined to "Hellenize" the story, to see everyone in trouble—not just Greece—as having gotten there through fiscal irresponsibility. And given that false belief, there's a natural turn to a false remedy: if fiscal profligacy was the problem, fiscal rectitude must be the solution. It's economics as morality play, with the extra twist that the sins being punished for the most part never happened.

But that's only part of the story. Europe's inability to come to grips with its real problems, and its insistence on confronting fake problems instead, is by no means unique. In 2010 much of the policy elite on both sides of the Atlantic fell head over heels for a related set of fallacies about debt, inflation, and growth. I'll try to explain these fallacies and also, a much harder task, why so many important people decided to endorse them, in the next chapter.

CHAPTER ELEVEN

AUSTERIANS

One cut after another: many economists say that there is a clear risk of deflation. What are your views on this?

I don't think that such risks could materialise. On the contrary, inflation expectations are remarkably well anchored in line with our definition—less than 2%, close to 2%—and have remained so during the recent crisis. As regards the economy, the idea that austerity measures could trigger stagnation is incorrect.

Incorrect?

Yes. In fact, in these circumstances, everything that helps to increase the confidence of households, firms and investors in the sustainability of public finances is good for the consolidation of growth and job creation. I firmly believe that in the current circumstances confidence-inspiring policies will foster and not hamper economic recovery, because confidence is the key factor today.

—Interview of Jean-Claude Trichet, president of the European Central Bank, by the Italian newspaper *La Repubblica*, June 2010

IN THE SCARY months that followed the fall of Lehman Brothers, just about all major governments agreed that the sudden collapse of private spending had to be offset, and they turned to expansionary fiscal and monetary policy—spending more, taxing less, and printing lots of monetary base—in an effort to limit the damage. In so doing, they were following the advice of standard textbooks; more important, they were following the hard-earned lessons of the Great Depression.

But a funny thing happened in 2010: much of the world's policy elite—the bankers and financial officials who define conventional wisdom—decided to throw out the textbooks and the lessons of history, and declare that down is up. That is, it quite suddenly became the fashion to call for spending cuts, tax hikes, and even higher interest rates even in the face of mass unemployment.

And I do mean suddenly: the dominance of believers in immediate austerity—"Austerians," as the financial analyst Rob Parenteau felicitously dubbed them—was already well established by the spring of 2010, when the Organization for Economic Cooperation and Development released its latest report on the economic outlook. The OECD is a Paris-based think tank funded by a club of advanced-country governments, which is why people sometimes refer to the economically advanced world simply as "the OECD," because membership in the club is more or less synonymous with advanced status. As such, it is of necessity a deeply conventional place, the kind of place where documents are negotiated paragraph by paragraph so as to avoid offending any of the major players.

And what was the advice this bellwether of conventional wisdom gave to America in the spring of 2010, with inflation low, unemployment very high, and the federal government's borrowing costs near a record low? That the U.S. government should immediately move to slash the budget deficit and that the Federal Reserve should raise short-term interest rates dramatically by the end of the year.

Fortunately, U.S. authorities didn't follow that advice. There was some "passive" fiscal tightening as the Obama stimulus faded out, but no wholesale shift to austerity. And the Fed not only kept rates low; it embarked on a program of bond purchases in an attempt to provide more oomph to the weak recovery. In Britain, however, an election placed power in the hands of a Conservative–Liberal Democrat coalition that took the OECD's advice to heart, imposing a program of preemptive spending cuts even though Britain, like America, faced both high unemployment and very low costs of borrowing.

Meanwhile, on the European continent, fiscal austerity became all the rage—and the European Central Bank began raising interest rates in early 2011, despite the deeply depressed state of the euro area economy and the absence of any convincing inflationary threat.

Nor was the OECD alone in demanding monetary and fiscal tightening even in the face of depression. Other international organizations, like the Basel-based Bank for International Settlements (BIS), joined in; so did influential economists like Chicago's Raghuram Rajan and influential business voices like Pimco's Bill Gross. Oh, and in America leading Republicans seized on the various arguments being made for austerity as justifications for their own advocacy of spending cuts and tight money. To be sure, some people and organizations bucked the trend—most notably and gratifyingly, the International Monetary Fund continued to be a voice for what I considered policy sanity. But I think it's fair to say that in 2010–11 what I, following the blogger Duncan Black, often call Very Serious People—people who express opinions that are regarded as sound by the influential and respectable—moved very strongly to the view that it was time to tighten, despite the absence of anything resembling full recovery from the financial crisis and its aftermath.

What was behind this sudden shift in policy fashions? Actually, that's a question that can be answered in two ways: we can try to look at the substantive arguments that were made on behalf of fiscal austerity and monetary tightening, or we can try to understand the motives of those who were so eager to turn away from the fight against unemployment.

In this chapter, I'll try to look at the issue both ways, but I'll look at the substance first.

There is, however, a problem in doing that: if you try to parse the arguments of the Austerians, you find yourself chasing an elusive moving target. On interest rates, in particular, I often felt as if the advocates of higher rates were playing Calvinball—the game in the comic strip *Calvin and Hobbes* in which the players are constantly making up new rules. The OECD, the BIS, and various economists and financial types seemed quite sure that interest rates needed to go up, but their explanations of just why they needed to go up kept changing. This changeability in turn suggested that the real motives for demanding tightening had little to do with an objective assessment of the economics. It also means that I can't offer a critique of "the" argument for austerity and higher rates; there were various arguments, not necessarily consistent with one another.

Let's start with the argument that has probably had the most force: fear—specifically, fear that nations that don't turn their backs on stimulus and move to austerity, even in the face of high unemployment, will find themselves confronting debt crises similar to that of Greece.

The Fear Factor

Austerianism didn't spring out of nowhere. Even in the months immediately following the fall of Lehman Brothers, some voices denounced the attempts to rescue major economies by engaging in deficit spending and rolling the printing presses. In the heat of the moment, however, these voices were largely drowned out by those calling for urgent expansionary action.

By late 2009, though, both financial markets and the world

economy had stabilized, so that the perceived urgency of action had declined. And then came the Greek crisis, which anti-Keynesians everywhere seized upon as an example of what would happen to the rest of us if we didn't follow the straight and narrow path of fiscal rectitude.

· I've already pointed out, in chapter 10, that the Greek debt crisis was sui generis even within Europe, that the other debt crisis countries within the euro area suffered debt crises as a result of the financial crisis, not the other way around. Meanwhile, nations that still have their own currencies have seen no hint of a Greek-style run on their government debt, even when—like the United States, but also Britain and Japan—they too have large debt and deficits.

But none of these observations seemed to matter in the policy debate. As the political scientist Henry Farrell puts it in a study of the rise and fall of Keynesian policies in the crisis, "The collapse of market confidence in Greece was interpreted as a parable of the risks of fiscal profligacy. States which got themselves into serious fiscal difficulties risked collapse in market confidence and perhaps indeed utter ruin."

Indeed, it became all the fashion for respectable people to issue apocalyptic warnings about imminent disaster if we didn't move immediately to cut the deficit. Erskine Bowles, the co-chairman—the *Democratic* co-chairman!—of a panel that was supposed to deliver a plan for long-term deficit reduction, testified to Congress in March 2011, a few months after the panel failed to reach agreement, and warned about a debt crisis any day now:

This problem is going to happen, like the former chairman of the Fed said or Moody's said, this is a problem we're going to have to face up to. It may be two years, you know, maybe a little less, maybe a little more, but if our bankers over there in Asia begin to believe that we're not going to be solid on our debt, that we're not going to be able to meet our obligations, just stop and think for a minute what happens if they just stop buying our debt.

What happens to interest rates and what happens to the U.S. economy? The markets will absolutely devastate us if we don't step up to this problem. The problem is real, the solutions are painful and we have to act.

His co-chairman, Alan Simpson, then weighed in with an assertion that it would happen in *less* than two years. Meanwhile, actual investors seemed not at all worried: interest rates on long-term U.S. bonds were low by historical standards as Bowles and Simpson spoke, and proceeded to fall to record lows over the course of 2011.

Three other points are worth mentioning. First, in early 2011 alarmists had a favorite excuse for the apparent contradiction between their dire warnings of imminent catastrophe and the persistence of low interest rates: the Federal Reserve, they claimed, was keeping rates artificially low by buying debt under its program of "quantitative easing." Rates would spike, they said, when that program ended in June. They didn't.

Second, the preachers of imminent debt crisis claimed vindication in August 2011, when Standard & Poor's, the rating agency, downgraded the U.S. government, taking away its AAA status. There were many pronouncements to the effect that "the market has spoken." But it wasn't the market that had spoken; it was just a rating agency—an agency that, like its peers, had given AAA ratings to many financial instruments that eventually turned into toxic waste. And the actual market's reaction to the S&P downgrade was . . . nothing. If anything, U.S. borrowing costs went down. As I mentioned in chapter 8, this came as no surprise to those economists who had studied Japan's experience: both S&P and its competitor Moody's downgraded Japan in 2002, at a time when the Japanese economy's situation resembled that of the United States in 2011, and nothing at all happened.

Finally, even if one took warnings about a looming debt crisis seriously, it was far from clear that immediate fiscal austerity—spending cuts and tax hikes when the economy was already deeply depressed—would help ward that crisis off. It's one thing to cut spending or raise taxes when the economy is fairly close to full employment, and the central bank is raising rates to head off the risk of inflation. In that situation, spending cuts need not depress the economy, because the central bank can offset their depressing effect by cutting, or at least not raising, interest rates. If the economy is deeply depressed, however, and interest rates are already near zero, spending cuts can't be offset. So they depress the economy further—and this reduces revenues, wiping out at least part of the attempted deficit reduction.

So even if you were worried about a potential loss of confidence, or at any rate worried about the long-term budget picture, economic logic would seem to suggest that austerity should wait—that there should be plans for longer-term cuts in spending and tax hikes, but that these cuts and hikes should not take effect until the economy was stronger.

But the Austerians rejected that logic, insisting that immediate cuts were necessary to restore confidence—and that restored confidence would make those cuts expansionary, not contractionary. This, then, brings us to a second strand of argument: the debate over the output and employment effects of austerity in a depressed economy.

The Confidence Fairy

I opened this chapter with remarks by Jean-Claude Trichet, the president of the European Central Bank until the fall of 2011, that encapsulate the remarkably optimistic—and remarkably foolish—doctrine that swept the corridors of power in 2010. This doctrine accepted the idea that the direct effect of slashing government spending is to reduce demand, which would, other things being equal, lead to an economic downturn and higher unemployment. But "confidence," people like Trichet insisted, would more than make up for this direct effect.

Early on, I took to calling this doctrine belief in the "confidence fairy," a coinage that seems to have stuck. But what was this all about? Is it possible that cutting government spending can actually increase demand? Yes, it is. In fact, there are a couple of channels through which spending cuts could in principle lead to higher demand: by reducing interest rates and/or by leading people to expect lower future taxes.

Here's how the interest rate channel would work: investors, impressed by a government's effort to reduce its budget deficit, would revise down their expectations about future government borrowing and hence about the future level of interest rates. Because long-term interest rates today reflect expectations about future rates, this expectation of lower future borrowing could lead to lower rates right away. And these lower rates could lead to higher investment spending right away.

Alternatively, austerity now might impress consumers: they could look at the government's enthusiasm for cutting and conclude that future taxes wouldn't be as high as they had been expecting. And their belief in a lower tax burden would make them feel richer and spend more, once again right away.

The question, then, wasn't whether it was possible for austerity to actually expand the economy through these channels; it was whether it was at all plausible to believe that favorable effects through either the interest rate or the expected tax channel would offset the direct depressing effect of lower government spending, particularly under current conditions.

To me, and to many other economists, the answer seemed clear: expansionary austerity was highly implausible in general, and especially given the state of the world as it was in 2010 and remains two years later. To repeat, the key point is that to justify statements like that made by Jean-Claude Trichet to *La Repubblica*, it's not enough for these confidence-related effects to *exist*; they have to be strong enough to more than offset the direct, depressing effects of austerity right now. That was hard to imagine for the interest rate channel, given that rates were already very low at the beginning of 2010 (and are even lower at the time of this writing). As for the effects via expected future taxes, how many people do you know who decide how much they can afford to spend this year by trying to estimate what current fiscal decisions will mean for their taxes five or ten years in the future?

Never mind, said the Austerians: we have strong empirical evidence for our claims. And thereby hangs a tale.

A decade before the crisis, back in 1998, the Harvard economist Alberto Alesina published a paper titled "Tales of Fiscal Adjustments," a study of countries that had moved to bring down large budget deficits. In that study he argued for strong confidence effects, so strong that in many cases austerity actually led to economic expansion. It was a striking conclusion, but one that at the time didn't attract as much interest—or as much critical examination—as one might have expected. In 1998 the general consensus among economists was still that the Fed and other central banks could always do what was necessary to stabilize the economy, so the effects of fiscal policy didn't seem that important one way or the other.

Matters were quite different, of course, by 2010, when the question of more stimulus versus austerity was central to economic policy debates. Advocates of austerity seized on Alesina's claim, as well as on a new paper, written with Silvia Ardagna, that tried to identify "large changes in fiscal policy" across a large sample of countries and time periods, and claimed to show many examples of expansionary austerity.

These claims were further buttressed by an appeal to historical examples. Look at Ireland in the late 1980s, they said, or Canada in the mid-1990s, or several other cases; these were countries that drastically reduced their budget deficits, and their economies boomed rather than slumping.

In normal times, the latest academic research plays a very small role in real-world policy debates, which is arguably how it should be—in the heat of the political moment, how many policy makers are truly equipped to evaluate the quality of a professor's statistical analysis? Better to leave time for the usual process of academic debate and scrutiny to sort out the solid from the spurious. But Alesina/Ardagna was immediately adopted and championed by policy makers and advocates around the world. That was unfortunate, because neither statistical results nor historical examples supposedly demonstrating expansionary austerity in practice held up well at all once people began looking at them closely.

How so? There were two key points: the problem of spurious correlation, and the fact that fiscal policy usually isn't the only game in town, but that it is right now.

On the first point, consider the example of the big U.S. move from budget deficit to budget surplus at the end of the 1990s. This move was associated with a booming economy; so was it a demonstration of expansionary austerity? No, it wasn't: both the boom and the fall in the deficit largely reflected a third factor, the technology boom and bubble, which helped propel the economy forward, but also caused soaring stock prices, which in turn translated into surging tax receipts. The correlation between the reduced deficit and the strong economy did not imply causation.

Now, Alesina and Ardagna corrected for one source of spurious correlation, the unemployment rate, but as people studying their paper quickly noticed, that wasn't enough. Their episodes of both fiscal austerity and fiscal stimulus didn't correspond at all closely to actual policy events—for example, they didn't catch either Japan's big stimulus effort in 1995 or its sharp turn to austerity in 1997.

Last year researchers at the IMF tried to deal with this problem by using direct information on policy changes to identify episodes of fiscal austerity. They found that fiscal austerity depresses the economy rather than expanding it.

Yet even this approach probably understated how "Keynesian" the world really is right now. Why? Because governments are usually able to take actions to offset the effects of budget austerity—in particular, cutting interest rates and/or devaluing their currencies—that aren't available for most troubled economies in the current depression.

Consider another example, Canada in the mid-1990s,

which sharply reduced its budget deficit in the mid-1990s while maintaining strong economic expansion. When the current government in Britain came to power, its officials liked to use the Canadian case to justify their belief that their austerity policies would not cause a sharp economic slowdown. But if you looked at what was going on in Canada at the time, you saw, first of all, that interest rates fell dramatically—something not possible in contemporary Britain, because rates are already very low. You also saw that Canada was able to sharply increase exports to its booming neighbor, the United States, thanks in part to a sharp decline in the value of the Canadian dollar. Again, this wasn't a feasible thing for Britain right now, since its neighbor—the euro area—is anything but booming, and the euro area's economic weakness is keeping its currency weak, too.

I could go on, but I've probably gone on too much already. The point is that the hoopla over the reported evidence for expansionary austerity was out of all proportion to the strength of that evidence. In fact, the case for believing in expansionary austerity quickly collapsed once serious scrutiny began. It's hard to avoid the conclusion that the policy elite eagerly embraced Alesina/Ardagna and the supposed lessons of history, without checking at all whether this evidence was solid, because these studies told members of that elite what they wanted to hear. Why was it what they wanted to hear? Good question. First, though, let's examine how one big experiment in austerity is going.

The British Experiment

For the most part, countries adopting harsh austerity policies despite high unemployment have done so under duress.

Greece, Ireland, Spain, and others found themselves unable to roll over their debts and were forced to slash spending and raise taxes to satisfy Germany and other governments providing emergency loans. But there has been one dramatic case of a government engaging in unforced austerity because it believed in the confidence fairy: Prime Minister David Cameron's government in Britain.

Cameron's hard-line policies were something of a political surprise. True, the Conservative Party had been preaching the austerity gospel before the 2010 British election. But it was able to form a government only through an alliance with the Liberal Democrats, whom one might have expected to be a moderating force. Instead, the Lib Dems were carried along by the Tories' zeal; soon after taking office, Cameron announced a program of dramatic spending cuts. And because Britain, unlike America, doesn't have a system in which a determined minority can hold up policies dictated from the top, the austerity program has gone into effect.

Cameron's policies were squarely based on concerns about confidence. Announcing his first budget after taking office, George Osborne, the chancellor of the exchequer, declared that without spending cuts, Britain would face

> higher interest rates, more business failures, sharper rises in unemployment, and potentially even a catastrophic loss of confidence and the end of the recovery. We cannot let that happen. This Budget is needed to deal with our country's debts. This Budget is needed to give confidence to our economy. This is the unavoidable Budget.

Cameron's policies were lauded both by conservatives and by self-styled centrists in the United States. For example, the

Washington Post's David Broder waxed rhapsodic: "Cameron and his partners in the coalition have pushed ahead boldly, brushing aside the warnings of economists that the sudden, severe medicine could cut short Britain's economic recovery and throw the nation back into recession."

So how's it going?

Well, British interest rates did stay low—but so did rates in the United States and Japan, which have even higher debt levels, but didn't make sharp turns to austerity. Basically, investors seem unworried about any advanced country with a stable government and its own currency.

What about the confidence fairy? Did consumers and business become more confident after Britain's turn to austerity? On the contrary, business confidence fell to levels not seen since the worst of the financial crisis, and consumer confidence fell even below the levels of 2008–09.

The result is an economy that remains deeply depressed. As the National Institute for Economic and Social Research, a British think tank, pointed out in a startling calculation, there is a real sense in which Britain is doing worse in this slump than it did in the Great Depression: by the fourth year after the Depression began, British GDP had regained its previous peak, but this time around it's still well below its level in early 2008.

And at the time of this writing, Britain seemed to be entering a new recession.

One could hardly have imagined a stronger demonstration that the Austerians had it wrong. Yet as I write this, Cameron and Osborne remain adamant that they will not change course.

The one good thing about the British scene is that the Bank of England, the equivalent of the Federal Reserve, has continued doing what it can to mitigate the slump. It deserves special praise for doing so, because quite a few voices have been demanding not just fiscal austerity but higher interest rates, too.

The Work of Depressions

The Austerian desire to slash government spending and reduce deficits even in the face of a depressed economy may be wrongheaded; indeed, my view is that it's deeply destructive. Still, it's not too hard to understand, since sustained deficits can be a real problem. The urge to raise interest rates is harder to understand. In fact, I was quite shocked when the OECD called for rate hikes in May of 2010, and it still seems to me to be a remarkable and strange call.

Why raise rates when the economy is deeply depressed and there seems to be little risk of inflation? The explanations keep shifting.

Back in 2010, when the OECD called for big rate increases, it did an odd thing: it contradicted its own economic forecast. That forecast, based on its models, showed low inflation and high unemployment for years to come. But financial markets, which were more optimistic at the time (they changed their mind later), were implicitly predicting some rise in inflation. The predicted inflation rates were still low by historical standards, but the OECD seized on the rise in predicted inflation to justify a call for tighter money.

By spring 2011, a spike in commodity prices had led to a rise in actual inflation, and the European Central Bank cited that rise as a reason to raise interest rates. That may sound reasonable, except for two things. First, it was quite obvious in the data that this was a temporary event driven by events outside of Europe, that there had been little change in underlying inflation, and that the rise in headline inflation was likely to reverse itself in the near future, as indeed it did. Second, the ECB famously overreacted to a temporary, commodity-driven bump in inflation back in 2008, raising interest rates just as the world economy was plunging into recession. Surely it wouldn't make exactly the same mistake just a few years later? But it did.

Why did the ECB act with such wrongheaded determination? The answer, I suspect, is that in the world of finance there was a general dislike of low interest rates that had nothing to do with inflation fears; inflation fears were invoked largely to support this preexisting desire to see interest rates rise.

Why would anyone want to raise rates despite high unemployment and low inflation? Well, there were a few attempts to provide a rationale, but they were confusing at best.

For example, Raghuram Rajan of the University of Chicago published an article in the *Financial Times* under the headline "Bernanke Must End Era of Ultra-low Rates." In it he warned that low rates might lead to "risk-taking and asset price inflation"—an odd thing to be worried about, given the clear and present problem of mass unemployment. But he also argued that unemployment was not of a kind that could be solved with higher demand—an argument I took on and, I hope, refuted in chapter 2—and went on,

The bottom line is that the current jobless recovery suggests the US has to undertake deep structural reforms to improve its supply side. The quality of its financial sector, its physical infrastructure, as well as its human capital, all need serious, and politically difficult, upgrades. If this is our goal, it is unwise to try to revive the patterns of demand before the recession, following the same monetary policies that led to disaster.

The idea that interest rates low enough to promote full employment would somehow be an obstacle to economic adjustment seems odd, but it also sounded familiar to those of us who had looked at the flailing of economists trying to come to grips with the Great Depression. In particular, Rajan's discussion closely echoed an infamous passage from Joseph Schumpeter, in which he warned against any remedial policies that might prevent the "work of depressions" from being achieved:

> In *all* cases, not only in the two which we have analyzed, recovery came of itself. There is certainly this much of truth in the talk about the recuperative powers of our industrial system. But this is not all: our analysis leads us to believe that recovery is sound only if it does come of itself. For any revival which is merely due to artificial stimulus leaves part of the work of depressions undone and adds, to an undigested remnant of maladjustment, new maladjustment of its own which has to be liquidated in turn, thus threatening business with another crisis ahead. Particularly, our story provides a *presumption* against remedial measures which work through money and credit. For the trouble is fundamentally *not* with money and credit, and policies of this class are particularly apt to keep up, and add to, maladjustment, and to produce additional trouble in the future.

When I studied economics, claims like Schumpeter's were described as characteristic of the "liquidationist" school, which basically asserted that the suffering that takes place in a depression is good and natural, and that nothing should be done to alleviate it. And liquidationism, we were taught, had been decisively refuted by events. Never mind Keynes; *Milton Friedman* had crusaded against this kind of thinking.

Yet in 2010 liquidationist arguments no different from those of Schumpeter (or Hayek) suddenly regained prominence. Rajan's writings provide the most explicit statement of the new liquidationism, but I have heard similar arguments from many financial officials. No new evidence or careful reasoning was presented to explain why this doctrine should rise from the dead. Why the sudden appeal?

At this point, I think we have to turn to the question of motivations. Why has Austerian doctrine been so appealing to Very Serious People?

Reasons Why

Early in his masterwork, *The General Theory of Employment, Interest, and Money,* John Maynard Keynes speculated about why the belief that economies could never suffer from inadequate demand, and that it was therefore wrong for governments ever to seek to increase demand—what he referred to as "Ricardian" economics, after the early nineteenth-century economist David Ricardo—had dominated respectable opinion for so long. His musings are as sharp and forceful now as when they were written:

> The completeness of the Ricardian victory is something of a curiosity and a mystery. It must have been due to a complex of suitabilities in the doctrine to the environment into which it was projected. That it reached conclusions quite different from what the ordinary uninstructed person would expect,

added, I suppose, to its intellectual prestige. That its teaching, translated into practice, was austere and often unpalat-
able, lent it virtue. That it was adapted to carry a vast and
consistent logical superstructure, gave it beauty. That it could
explain much social injustice and apparent cruelty as an inevitable incident in the scheme of progress, and the attempt to
change such things as likely on the whole to do more harm
than good, commended it to authority. That it afforded a
measure of justification to the free activities of the individual
capitalist, attracted to it the support of the dominant social
force behind authority.

Indeed; the part about how the economic doctrine that
demands austerity also rationalizes social injustice and cruelty
more broadly, and how this recommends it to authority, rings
especially true.

We might add an insight from another twentieth-century
economist, Michal Kalecki, who wrote a penetrating 1943 essay
on the importance to business leaders of the appeal to "confidence." As long as there are no routes back to full employment except that of somehow restoring business confidence,
he pointed out, business lobbies in effect have veto power over
government actions: propose doing anything they dislike, such
as raising taxes or enhancing workers' bargaining power, and
they can issue dire warnings that this will reduce confidence
and plunge the nation into depression. But let monetary and
fiscal policy be deployed to fight unemployment, and suddenly
business confidence becomes less necessary, and the need to
cater to capitalists' concerns is much reduced.

Let me add yet another line of explanation. If you look at
what Austerians want—fiscal policy that focuses on deficits

rather than on job creation, monetary policy that obsessively fights even the hint of inflation and raises interest rates even in the face of mass unemployment—all of it in effect serves the interests of creditors, of those who lend as opposed to those who borrow and/or work for a living. Lenders want governments to make honoring their debts the highest priority; and they oppose any action on the monetary side that either deprives bankers of returns by keeping rates low or erodes the value of claims through inflation.

Finally, there's the continuing urge to make the economic crisis a morality play, a tale in which a depression is the necessary consequence of prior sins and must not be alleviated. Deficit spending and low interest rates just seem *wrong* to many people, perhaps especially to central bankers and other financial officials, whose sense of self-worth is bound up with the idea of being the grown-ups who say no.

The trouble is that in the current situation, insisting on perpetuating suffering isn't the grown-up, mature thing to do. It's both childish (judging policy by how it feels, not what it does) and destructive.

So what, specifically, should we be doing? And how can we get a change of course? That will be the subject of the remainder of this book.

CHAPTER TWELVE

WHAT IT WILL TAKE

*The outstanding faults of the economic society in which we live are
its failure to provide for full employment and its arbitrary and ineq-
uitable distribution of wealth and incomes.*

— John Maynard Keynes, *The General Theory of
Employment, Interest, and Money*

AS IT WAS in 1936, so it is today. Now, as then, our society
is blighted by mass unemployment. Now, as then, the lack of
jobs represents a failure of a system that was hugely unequal
and unjust even in "good times."

Should the fact that we've been here before be a source of
despair or of hope? I vote for hope. After all, we did eventually
cure the problems that caused the Great Depression, and created a much more equal society too. You may lament that the
fix didn't last forever, but then nothing does (except red wine
stains on a white couch). The fact is that we had almost two
generations of more or less adequate employment and tolerable
levels of inequality after World War II, and we can do it again.

Narrowing income gaps will be a difficult task, and will probably have to be a long-term project. It's true that the last time around income inequality was reduced very quickly, in the so-called "great compression" of the war years; but since we aren't about to have a war economy with all the controls that implies—or at least I hope we aren't—it's probably unrealistic to expect a quick solution.

The problem of unemployment, however, is not a hard one in purely economic terms, nor need the cure take a long time. Between 1939 and 1941—that is, before the attack on Pearl Harbor and America's actual entry into war—a burst of federal spending caused a 7 percent rise in the total number of jobs in America, the equivalent of adding more than ten million jobs today. You may say that this time is different, but one of the main messages of this book is that it isn't; there is no good reason why we could not repeat that achievement if only we had the intellectual clarity and political will. Every time you hear some talking head declare that we have a long-term problem that can't be solved with short-term fixes, you should know that while he may think he sounds wise, he's actually being both cruel and foolish. This depression could and should be ended very quickly.

By now, if you've been reading this book from the beginning, you should have a pretty good idea of what a depression-ending strategy should involve. In this chapter I'll lay it out more explicitly. Before I get there, however, let me take a moment to deal with claims that the economy is already healing itself.

Things Are Not OK

I'm writing these words in February 2012, not long after a jobs report came out that was better than expected. In fact, for the past several months we've been getting somewhat encouraging news on jobs: employment is growing fairly solidly, measured unemployment is falling, new claims for unemployment insurance are down, optimism is rising.

And it may be that the natural recuperative powers of the economy are starting to kick in. Even John Maynard Keynes argued that these recuperative powers exist, that over time "use, decay and obsolescence" eat away at the existing stock of buildings and machines, eventually causing a "scarcity" of capital that induces businesses to start investing and thereby start a process of recovery. We might add that the burden of household debt is inching down too, as some families manage to pay off their debt and as other debts are canceled by default. So has the need for action passed?

No, it hasn't.

For one thing, this is actually the *third* time many people have sounded the all-clear on the economy. After Bernanke's "green shoots" in 2009 and the Obama administration's "recovery summer" in 2010, surely we want more than a few months of better data before declaring victory.

The really important thing to understand, however, is how deep a hole we're in and how small the recent climb. Let me offer one gauge of where we are: the employed fraction of prime-working-age adults, shown on page 211. In using this measure, I don't mean to suggest that the availability of jobs for younger and older Americans is unimportant; I'm just choosing a labor market indicator that isn't affected by trends like an aging population, so that it's consistent over time. What it shows is that, yes, there has been some improvement in the past few months—but that improvement looks almost pitiful compared with the crash that took place in 2008 and 2009.

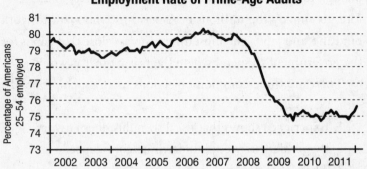

Employment Rate of Prime-Age Adults

There have been signs of an improving employment picture recently, but we're still deep in the hole.

Source: Bureau of Labor Statistics

And even if the recent good news continues, how long will it take to restore full employment? A very long time. I haven't seen any plausible estimate that puts the time to full recovery at less than five years, and something more like seven years is probably a better number.

This is a terrible prospect. Every month that this depression goes on inflicts continuing and cumulative damage on our society, damage measured not just in present pain but in a degraded future. If there are things we can do to accelerate recovery dramatically—and there are—we should do them.

But, you say, what about the political obstacles? They are, of course, real, but maybe not as impassable as many people imagine. In this chapter I want to put politics on one side, and talk about the three main areas in which policy could make a huge difference, starting with government spending.

Spend Now, Pay Later

The basic situation of the U.S. economy remains now what it has been since 2008: the private sector isn't willing to spend enough to make use of our full productive capacity and, therefore, to employ the millions of Americans who want to work but can't find jobs. The most direct way to close that gap is for the government to spend where the private sector won't.

There are three common objections to any such proposal:

1. Experience shows that fiscal stimulus doesn't work.
2. Bigger deficits would undermine confidence.
3. There aren't enough good projects to spend on.

I've dealt with the first two objections earlier in this book; let me briefly summarize the arguments again, then turn to the third.

As I explained in chapter 7, the Obama stimulus didn't fail; it simply fell short of what was required to offset the huge private-sector pullback that was already under way before the stimulus kicked in. Continuing high unemployment was not just predictable but predicted.

The real evidence we should be considering here is the rapidly growing body of economic research on the effects of changes in government spending on output and employment— a body of research that relies both on "natural experiments" such as wars and defense buildups and on careful study of the historical record to identify major changes in fiscal policy. The postscript to this book summarizes some of the major contributions to this research. What the work says, clearly and overwhelmingly, is that changes in government spending move output and employment in the same direction: spend more, and both real GDP and employment will rise; spend less, and both real GDP and employment will fall.

What about confidence? As I explained in chapter 8, there's

no reason to believe that even a substantial stimulus would undermine the willingness of investors to buy U.S. bonds. In fact, bond market confidence might even rise on the prospect of faster growth. Meanwhile, both consumer and business confidence would actually rise if policy turned to boosting the real economy.

The last objection, about what to spend on, has more force. A perceived lack of good "shovel-ready" projects was a real concern back when the original Obama stimulus was being devised. I would argue, however, that even then the constraints on spending weren't as tight as many officials imagined—and at this point it would be relatively easy to achieve a large temporary rise in spending. Why? Because we could give the economy a large boost just by reversing the destructive austerity that has already been imposed by state and local governments.

I've mentioned this austerity before, but it really becomes crucial when you think of what we could do in the short run to help our economy. Unlike the federal government, state and local governments are more or less required to balance their budgets each year, which means that they must slash spending and/or raise taxes when recession strikes. The Obama stimulus included a significant amount of aid to states intended to help avoid these economy-depressing actions, but the money was insufficient even in the first year, and it has long since run out. The result has been a major pullback, illustrated by the figure on page 214, which shows employment by state and local governments. At this point the number of workers in those governments is down by more than half a million, with the majority of the job losses coming from the area of education.

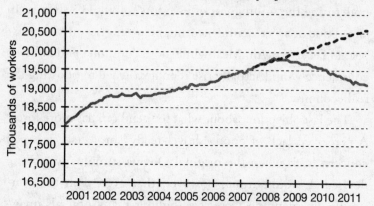

State and Local Government Employment

Employment at lower levels of government has fallen sharply, when it should have been growing with population, leaving a shortfall of more than a million workers, many of them schoolteachers.

Source: Bureau of Labor Statistics

Now ask what would have happened if states and local governments had not been forced into austerity. Clearly, they wouldn't have laid off all those schoolteachers; in fact, their workforces would have continued to grow, if only to serve a larger population. The dashed line shows what would have happened to state and local government employment if it had continued to grow in line with population, around 1 percent a year. This rough calculation suggests that if adequate federal aid had been provided, these lower level governments might now be employing around 1.3 million more workers than they actually are. A similar analysis on the spending side suggests that if it hadn't been for severe budget constraints, state and local governments would be spending perhaps $300 billion a year more than they actually are.

So right there is a stimulus of $300 billion per year that

could be accomplished simply by providing enough aid to states and localities to let them reverse their recent budget cuts. It would create well over a million jobs directly and probably something like three million once you take the indirect effects into account. And it could be done quickly, since we're talking only about restoring cuts rather than about initiating new projects.

That said, there should be new projects too. They don't have to be visionary projects like ultra-high-speed rail; they can be mainly prosaic investments in roads, rail upgrades, water systems, and so on. One effect of the forced austerity at the state and local level has been a sharp drop in spending on infrastructure, representing delayed or canceled projects, deferred maintenance, and the like. It should thus be possible to get a significant burst in spending just by restarting all the things that were postponed or canceled these past few years.

But what if some of these projects end up taking a while to get going, and the economy has fully recovered before they're finished? The appropriate answer is, so? It has been obvious from the beginning of this depression that the risks of doing too little are much bigger than the risks of doing too much. If government spending threatens to lead to an overheated economy, this is a problem the Federal Reserve can easily contain by raising interest rates a bit faster than it might have otherwise. What we should have feared all along is what actually happened, with government spending inadequate to the task of promoting job creation, and the Fed unable to cut rates because they're already zero.

That said, there is more the Fed could and should be doing, which I'll get to in a moment. First, however, let me add that there is at least one more channel through which government spending could provide a fairly quick boost to the economy: more aid to distressed individuals, by means of a temporary increase in the generosity of unemployment insurance and other safety net programs. There was some of this in the original stimulus, but not enough, and it faded out far too fast. Put money in the hands of people in distress, and there's a good chance they'll spend it, which is exactly what we need to see happen.

So the technical obstacles to a major new fiscal stimulus—a major new program of government spending to boost the economy—are much less than many people seem to imagine. We can do this; and it will work even better if the Fed does more, too.

The Fed

Japan entered a prolonged slump in the early 1990s, a slump from which it has never fully emerged. That represented a huge failure of economic policy, and outsiders were not shy about pointing that out. For example, in 2000 one prominent Princeton economist published a paper harshly criticizing the Bank of Japan, Japan's equivalent of the Federal Reserve, for not taking stronger action. The BoJ, he asserted, was suffering from "self-inflicted paralysis." Aside from suggesting a number of specific actions the BoJ should take, he made the general case that it should do whatever it took to generate a strong economic recovery.

The professor's name, as some readers may have guessed, was Ben Bernanke, who now heads the Fed—and whose institution seems to suffer from the very self-induced paralysis he once decried in others.

Like the BoJ in 2000, the Fed today can no longer use conventional monetary policy, which works through changes in short-term interest rates, to give the economy a further boost, because those rates are already zero and can go no lower. But back then Professor Bernanke argued that there were other measures monetary authorities could take that would be effective even with short-term rates up against the "zero lower bound." Among the measures were the following:

- Using newly printed money to buy "unconventional" assets like long-term bonds and private debts
- Using newly printed money to pay for temporary tax cuts
- Setting targets for long-term interest rates—for example, pledging to keep the interest rate on ten-year bonds below 2.5 percent for four or five years, if necessary by having the Fed buy these bonds
- Intervening in the foreign exchange market to push the value of your currency down, strengthening the export sector
- Setting a higher target for inflation, say 3 or 4 percent, for the next five or even ten years

Bernanke pointed out that there was a substantial body of economic analysis and evidence for the proposition that each of these policies would have a real positive effect on growth and employment. (The inflation-target idea actually came from a paper I published in 1998.) He also argued that the details probably weren't all that important, that what was really needed was "Rooseveltian resolve," a "willingness to be aggressive and experiment—in short, to do whatever was necessary to get the country moving again."

Unfortunately, Chairman Bernanke hasn't followed Professor Bernanke's advice. To be fair, the Fed has moved to some extent on the first bullet point above: under the deeply confusing name of "quantitative easing," it has bought both longer-term government debt and mortgage-backed securities. But there has been no hint of Rooseveltian resolve to do whatever is necessary: rather than being aggressive and experimental, the Fed has tiptoed up to quantitative easing, doing it now and then when the economy looks especially weak, but quickly ending its efforts whenever the news picks up a bit.

Why has the Fed been so timid, given that its chairman's own writings suggest that it should be doing much more? One answer may be that it has been intimidated by political pressure: Republicans in Congress went wild over quantitative easing, accusing Bernanke of "debasing the dollar"; Rick Perry, the governor of Texas, famously warned that something "ugly" might happen to Bernanke if he visited the Lone Star State.

But that may not be the whole story. Laurence Ball of Johns Hopkins University, a distinguished macroeconomist in his own right, has studied the evolution of Bernanke's views over the years as revealed by the minutes of Federal Reserve meetings. If I had to summarize Ball's analysis, I would say that he suggests that Bernanke was assimilated by the Fed Borg, that the pressures of groupthink and the lure of camaraderie pushed Bernanke over time into a position that gave higher priority to keeping the Fed's goals modest, thereby making life easier for the institution, than to helping the economy by any means necessary. The sad irony is that back in 2000 Bernanke criticized the Bank of Japan for essentially having the same attitude, of being unwilling to "try anything that isn't absolutely guaranteed to work."

Whatever the reasons for the Fed's passivity, the point I want to make right now is that all the possible actions Professor Bernanke suggested for a time like this, but which Chairman Bernanke has not, in fact, tried, remain available. Joseph Gagnon, a former Fed official now at the Peterson Institute for International Economics, has laid out a specific plan for much more aggressive quantitative easing; the Fed should move ahead with that plan or something like it right away. It should also commit to modestly higher inflation, say, 4 percent over the next five years—or, alternatively, set a target for the dollar value of GDP that would imply a similar rate of inflation. And it should stand ready to do more if this proves insufficient.

Would such aggressive Fed actions work? Not necessarily, but as Bernanke himself used to argue, the point is to try, and keep on trying if the first round proves inadequate. Aggressive Fed action would be especially likely to work if accompanied by the kind of fiscal stimulus I described above—and also if accompanied by strong action on housing, the third leg of a recovery strategy.

Housing

Since a large part of our economic troubles can be attributed to the debt home buyers ran up during the bubble years, one obvious way to improve the situation would be to reduce the burden of that debt. Yet attempts to provide homeowner relief have been, to put it bluntly, a total bust. Why? Mainly, I'd argue, because both the plans for relief and their implementation have been crippled by fear that some undeserving debtors might receive relief, and that this would provoke a political backlash.

So in keeping with the principle of Rooseveltian resolve,

aka "If at first you don't succeed, try, try again," we should try debt relief again, this time based on the understanding that the economy badly needs such relief, and that this should trump concerns that some of the benefits of relief might flow to people who behaved irresponsibly in the past.

Yet even that is not the whole story. I noted above that severe cutbacks by state and local governments have, in a perverse way, made fiscal stimulus an easier proposition than it was in early 2009, since we could get a major boost just from reversing those cuts. In a somewhat different way, the prolonged economic slump has also made housing relief easier. For the depressed economy has led to depressed interest rates, including mortgage rates: conventional mortgages taken out at the height of the mortgage boom often had rates above 6 percent, but those rates are now below 4 percent.

Ordinarily, homeowners would take advantage of this fall in rates to refinance, reducing their interest payments and freeing up funds that could be spent on other things, boosting the economy. But the legacy of the bubble is a large number of homeowners with very little equity in their homes, or in quite a few cases negative equity—their mortgages are larger than the market value of their houses. And in general lenders won't approve a refinancing unless the borrower has sufficient home equity or is able to put up an additional down payment.

The solution would seem to be obvious: find a way to waive or at least soften these rules. And the Obama administration has in fact had a program, the Home Affordable Refinance Program, with that goal. But like previous housing policies, HARP has been far too cautious and restrictive. What is needed is a program of mass refinancing—something that should be easier because many mortgages are owed to Fannie and Freddie, which are now fully nationalized.

This isn't happening yet, in part because the head of the Federal Housing Finance Agency, which oversees Fannie and Freddie, is dragging his feet. (He's a presidential appointee— but Obama apparently isn't willing to just tell him what to do, and fire him if he won't.) But that means that the opportunity is still out there. Furthermore, as Joseph Gagnon of the Peterson Institute points out, a mass refinancing could be especially effective if accompanied by an aggressive effort on the part of the Fed to drive down mortgage interest rates.

Refinancing wouldn't do away with the need for further debt-relief measures, just as reversing state and local austerity wouldn't eliminate the need for additional fiscal stimulus. The point, however, is that in both cases the changes in the economic situation over the past three years have opened up opportunities for some technically easy yet surprisingly major actions to boost our economy.

And More

The list of policies above isn't meant to be exhaustive. There are other fronts on which policy could and should move, notably foreign trade: it's long past time to take a tougher line on China and other currency manipulators, and sanction them if necessary. Even environmental regulation could play a positive role: by announcing targets for much-needed curbs on particulate emissions and greenhouse gases, with the rules to phase in gradually over time, the government could provide an incentive for businesses to spend on environmental upgrades now, helping accelerate economic recovery.

Without question, some of the policy measures I've described here will, if tried, not work as well as we might hope. But others will work better than we expect. What's crucial, beyond any specifics, is a determination to do something, to pursue policies for job creation and to keep trying until the goal of full employment has been achieved.

And the hints of good news in recent economic data if anything reinforce the case for aggressive action. It looks, to my eyes at least, as if the U.S. economy may be on the cusp: the economic engine might be on the verge of catching, self-sustaining growth might be about to get established—but that is by no means guaranteed. So this is very much a time to step on the gas pedal, not take our foot off it.

The big question, of course, is whether anyone in a position of power can or will take the advice of those of us pleading for more action. Won't politics and political discord stand in the way?

Yes, they will—but that's no reason to give up. And that's the subject of my final chapter.

CHAPTER THIRTEEN

END THIS DEPRESSION!

BY NOW, I HOPE I have convinced at least some readers that the depression we're in is essentially gratuitous: we don't need to be suffering so much pain and destroying so many lives. Moreover, we could end this depression both more easily and more quickly than anyone imagines—anyone, that is, except those who have actually studied the economics of depressed economies and the historical evidence on how policies work in such economies.

Yet I'm sure that, by the end of the last chapter, even sympathetic readers were starting to wonder whether all the economic analysis in the world can do any real good. Isn't a recovery program along the lines I've described just out of the question as a political matter? And isn't advocating such a program a waste of time?

My answer to these two questions is, not necessarily, and definitely not. The chances of a real turn in policy, away from the austerity mania of the last few years and toward a renewed focus on job creation, are much better than conventional wisdom would have you believe. And recent experience also teaches us a crucial political lesson: it's much better to stand up for what you believe, to make the case for what really should be done, than to try to seem moderate and reasonable by essentially accepting your opponents' arguments. Compromise, if you must, on the policy—but never on the truth.

Let me start by talking about the possibility of a decisive change in policy direction.

Nothing Succeeds like Success

Pundits are always making confident statements about what the American electorate wants and believes, and such presumed public views are often used to wave away any suggestion of major policy changes, at least from the left. America is a "center-right country," we're told, and that rules out any major initiatives involving new government spending.

And to be fair, there are lines, both to the left and to the right, that policy probably can't cross without inviting electoral disaster. George W. Bush discovered that when he tried to privatize Social Security after the 2004 election: the public hated the idea, and his attempted juggernaut on the issue quickly stalled. A comparably liberal-leaning proposal—say, a plan to introduce true "socialized medicine," making the whole health care system a government program like the Veterans Health Administration—would presumably experience the same fate. But when it comes to the kind of policy measures we're talking about here—measures that would mainly try to boost the economy rather than trying to transform it—public opinion is surely less coherent and less decisive than everyday commentary would have you believe.

Pundits and, I'm sorry to say, White House political operatives like to tell elaborate tales about what is supposedly going on in voters' minds. Back in 2011 the *Washington Post*'s Greg Sargent summarized the arguments Obama aides were using to justify a focus on spending cuts rather than job creation: "A big deal would reassure independents who fear the country is out of control; position Obama as the adult who made Washington work again; allow the President to tell Dems he put entitlements on sounder financial footing; and clear the decks to enact other priorities later."

Well, talk to any political scientist who has actually studied electoral behavior, and he or she will scoff at the idea that voters engage in anything like this sort of complicated reasoning. And political scientists in general have scorn for what *Slate*'s Matthew Yglesias calls the pundit's fallacy, the belief on the part of all too many political commentators that their pet issues are, miraculously, the very same issues that matter most to the electorate. Real voters are busy with their jobs, their children, and their lives in general. They have neither the time nor the inclination to study policy issues closely, let alone engage in opinion-page-style parsing of political nuances. What they notice, and vote on, is whether the economy is getting better or worse; statistical analyses say that the rate of economic growth in the three quarters or so before the election is by far the most important determinant of electoral outcomes.

What this says—a lesson that the Obama team unfortunately failed to learn until very late in the game—is that the economic strategy that works best politically isn't the strategy that finds approval with focus groups, let alone with the editorial page of the *Washington Post*; it's the strategy that actually delivers results. Whoever is sitting in the White House next year will best serve his own political interests by doing the right thing from an economic point of view, which means doing whatever it takes to end the depression we're in. If expansionary fiscal and monetary policies coupled with debt relief are the way to get this economy moving—and I hope I've convinced at least some readers that they are—then those policies will be politically smart as well as in the national interest.

But is there any chance of actually getting them enacted as legislation?

Political Possibilities

There will, of course, be a U.S. election in November, and it's not at all clear what the political landscape will look like after it. There do, however, seem to be three main possibilities: President Obama is reelected, and Democrats also regain control of Congress; a Republican, probably Mitt Romney, wins the presidential election, and Republicans add a Senate majority to their control of the House; the president is reelected, but faces at least one hostile house of Congress. What can be done in each of these cases?

The first case—Obama triumphant—obviously makes it easiest to imagine America doing what it takes to restore full employment. In effect, the Obama administration would get an opportunity at a do-over, taking the strong steps it failed to take in 2009. Since Obama is unlikely to have a filibuster-proof majority in the Senate, taking these strong steps would require making use of reconciliation, the procedure that the Democrats used to pass health care reform and that Bush used to pass both of his tax cuts. So be it. If nervous advisers warn about the political fallout, Obama should remember the hard-learned lesson of his first term: the best economic strategy from a political point of view is the one that delivers tangible progress.

A Romney victory would naturally create a very different situation; if Romney adhered to Republican orthodoxy, he would of course reject any action along the lines I've advocated.

It's not clear, however, whether Romney believes any of the things he is currently saying. His two chief economic advisers, Harvard's N. Gregory Mankiw and Columbia's Glenn Hubbard, are committed Republicans but also quite Keynesian in their views about macroeconomics. Indeed, early in the crisis Mankiw argued for a sharp rise in the Fed's inflation target, a proposal that was and is anathema to most of his party. His proposal caused the predictable uproar, and he went silent on the issue. But we can at least hope that Romney's inner circle holds views that are much more realistic than anything the candidate says in his speeches, and that once in office he would rip off his mask, revealing his true pragmatic/Keynesian nature.

I know, I know, hoping that a politician is in fact a complete fraud who doesn't believe any of the things he claims to believe is no way to run a great nation. And it's certainly not a reason to vote for that politician! Still, making the case for job creation may not be a wasted effort, even if Republicans take it all this November.

Finally, what about the fairly likely case in which Obama is returned to office but a Democratic Congress is not? What should Obama do, and what are the prospects for action? My answer is that the president, other Democrats, and every Keynesian-

minded economist with a public profile, should make the case
for job creation forcefully and often, and keep pressure on those
in Congress who are blocking job-creation efforts.

This is not the way the Obama administration operated for
its first two and a half years. We now have a number of reports
on the internal decision processes of the administration from
2009 to 2011, and they all suggest that the president's political
advisers urged him never to ask for things he might not get,
on the grounds that it might make him look weak. Moreover, economic advisers like Christy Romer who urged more
spending on job creation were overruled on the grounds that
the public didn't believe in such measures and was worried
about the deficit.

The result of this caution was, however, that as even the
president bought into deficit obsession and calls for austerity,
the whole national discourse shifted away from job creation.
Meanwhile, the economy remained weak—and the public had
no reason not to blame the president, since he wasn't staking
out a position clearly different from that of the GOP.

In September 2011 the White House finally changed tack,
offering a job-creation proposal that fell far short of what I
called for in chapter 12, but was nonetheless much bigger than
expected. There was no chance that the plan would actually
pass the Republican-led House of Representatives, and Noam
Scheiber of the *New Republic* tells us that White House political operatives "began to worry that the size of the package
would be a liability and urged the wonks to scale it back." This
time, however, Obama sided with the economists—and in the
process proved that the political operatives didn't know their
own business. Public reaction was generally favorable, while
Republicans were put on the spot for their obstruction.

And early this year, with the debate having shifted perceptibly toward a renewed focus on jobs, Republicans were on the defensive. As a result, the Obama administration was able to get a significant fraction of what it wanted—an extension of the payroll tax credit, which helps put cash in workers' pockets, and a shorter extension of extended unemployment benefits—without making any major concessions.

In short, the experience of Obama's first term suggests that not talking about jobs simply because you don't think you can pass job-creation legislation doesn't work even as a political strategy. On the other hand, hammering on the need for job creation can be good politics, and it can put enough pressure on the other side to bring about better policy too.

Or to put it more simply, there is no reason not to tell the truth about this depression—which brings me back to where this book started.

A Moral Imperative

So here we are, more than four years after the U.S. economy first entered recession—and although the recession may have ended, the depression has not. Unemployment may be trending down a bit in the United States (though it's rising in Europe), but it remains at levels that would have been inconceivable not long ago—and are unconscionable now. Tens of millions of our fellow citizens are suffering vast hardship, the future prospects of today's young people are being eroded with each passing month—and all of it is unnecessary.

For the fact is that we have both the knowledge and the tools to get out of this depression. Indeed, by applying time-honored economic principles whose validity has only been reinforced by recent events, we could be back to more or less full employment very fast, probably in less than two years.

All that is blocking recovery is a lack of intellectual clarity and political will. And it's the job of everyone who can make a difference, from professional economists, to politicians, to concerned citizens, to do whatever he or she can to remedy that lack. We can end this depression—and we need to fight for policies that will do the trick, starting right now.

WHAT DO WE REALLY KNOW ABOUT THE EFFECTS OF GOVERNMENT SPENDING?

ONE MAIN THEME of this book has been that in a deeply depressed economy, in which the interest rates that the monetary authorities can control are near zero, we need more, not less, government spending. A burst of federal spending is what ended the Great Depression, and we desperately need something similar today.

But how do we know that more government spending would actually promote growth and employment? After all, many politicians fiercely reject that idea, insisting that the government can't create jobs; some economists are willing to say the same thing. So is it just a question of going with the people who seem to be part of your political tribe?

Well, it shouldn't be. Tribal allegiance should have no more to do with your views about macroeconomics than with your views on, say, the theory of evolution or climate change . . . hmm, maybe I'd better stop right there.

Anyway, the point is that the question of how the economy works should be settled on the basis of evidence, not prejudice. And one of the few benefits of this depression has been a surge in evidence-based economic research into the effects of changes in government spending. What does that evidence say?

Before I can answer that question, I have to talk briefly about the pitfalls one needs to avoid.

The Trouble with Correlation

You might think that the way to assess the effects of government spending on the economy is simply to look at the correlation between spending levels and other things, like growth and employment. The truth is that even people who should know better sometimes fall into the trap of equating correlation with causation (see the discussion of debt and growth in chapter 8). But let me try to disabuse you of the notion that this is a useful procedure, by talking about a related question: the effects of tax rates on economic performance.

As you surely know, it's an article of faith on the American right that low taxes are the key to economic success. But suppose we look at the relationship between taxes—specifically, the share of GDP collected in federal taxes—and unemployment over the past dozen years. What we see is the following:

Year	Tax share (%)	Unemployment rate (%)
2000	20.6	4.0
2003	16.2	6.0
2007	18.5	4.6
2010	15.1	9.6

So years with high tax shares were years of low unemployment, and vice versa. Clearly, the way to reduce unemployment is to raise taxes!

OK, even those of us who very much disagree with tax-cut mania don't believe this. Why not? Because we're surely looking at spurious correlation here. For example, unemployment was relatively low in 2007 because the economy was still being buoyed by the housing boom—and the combination of a strong economy and large capital gains boosted federal revenues, making taxes look high. By 2010 the boom had gone bust, taking both the economy and tax receipts with it. Measured tax levels were a consequence of other things, not an independent variable driving the economy.

Similar problems bedevil any attempt to use historical correlations to assess the effects of government spending. If economics were a laboratory science, we could solve the problem by performing controlled experiments. But it isn't. Econometrics—a specialized branch of statistics that's supposed to help deal with such situations—offers a variety of techniques for "identifying" actual causal relationships. The truth, however, is that even economists are rarely persuaded by fancy econometric analyses, especially when the issue at hand is so politically charged. What, then, can be done?

The answer in much recent work has been to look for "natural experiments"—situations in which we can be pretty sure that changes in government spending are neither responding to economic developments nor being driven by forces that are also moving the economy through other channels. Where do such natural experiments come from? Sadly, they mainly come from disasters—wars or the threat of wars, and fiscal crises that force governments to slash spending regardless of the state of the economy.

Disasters, Guns, and Money

As I said, since the crisis began there has been a boom in research into the effects of fiscal policy on output and employment. This body of research is growing fast, and much of it is too technical to be summarized here. But here are a few highlights.

First, Stanford's Robert Hall has looked at the effects of large changes in U.S. government purchases—which is all about wars, specifically World War II and the Korean War. The figure on page 235 compares changes in U.S. military spending with changes in real GDP—both measured as a percentage of the preceding year's GDP—over the period from 1929 to 1962 (there's not much action after that). Each dot represents one year; I've labeled the points corresponding to the big buildup during World War II and the big demobilization just afterward. Obviously, there were big moves in years when nothing much was happening to military spending, notably the slump from 1929 to 1933 and the recovery from 1933 to 1936. But every year in which there was a big spending increase was also a year of strong growth, and the reduction in military spending after World War II was a year of sharp output decline.

This clearly suggests that increasing government spending does indeed create growth and hence jobs. The next question is, how much bang is there per buck? The data on U.S. military spending are slightly disappointing in that respect, suggesting that a dollar of spending actually generates only about $0.50 of growth. But if you know anything about wartime history, you realize that this may not be a good guide to what would happen if we increased spending now. After all, during World

Government Spending and Growth, 1929–1962

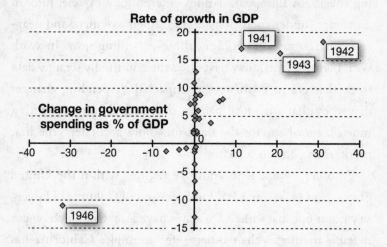

Big rises and falls in government spending centered on World War II and the Korean War were associated with corresponding booms and busts in the economy as a whole.

Source: Bureau of Economic Analysis

War II private-sector spending was deliberately suppressed by rationing and restrictions on private construction; during the Korean War, the government tried to avoid inflationary pressures by sharply raising taxes. So it's likely that an increase in spending now would yield bigger gains.

How much bigger? To answer that question, it would be helpful to find natural experiments telling us about the effects of government spending under conditions more like those we face today. Unfortunately, there aren't any such experiments as good and clear-cut as World War II. Still, there are some useful ways to get at the issue.

One is to go deeper into the past. As the economic histo-

rians Barry Eichengreen and Kevin O'Rourke point out, during the 1930s European nations entered, one by one, into an
arms race, under conditions of high unemployment and near-
zero interest rates resembling those prevailing now. In work
with their students, they have used the admittedly scrappy data
from that era to estimate the impact that spending changes
driven by that arms race had on output, and come up with a
much bigger bang for the buck (or, more accurately, the lira,
mark, franc, and so on).

Another option is to compare regions within the United
States. Emi Nakamura and Jon Steinsson of Columbia University point out that some U.S. states have long had much bigger
defense industries than others—for example, California has
long had a large concentration of defense contractors, whereas
Illinois has not. Meanwhile, defense spending at the national
level has fluctuated a lot, rising sharply under Reagan, then
falling after the end of the Cold War. At the national level, the
effects of these changes are obscured by other factors, especially monetary policy: the Fed raised rates sharply in the early
1980s, just as the Reagan buildup was occurring, and cut them
sharply in the early 1990s. But you can still get a good sense of
the impact of government spending by looking at the differential effect across states; Nakamura and Steinsson estimate, on
the basis of this differential, that a dollar of spending actually
raises output by around $1.50.

So looking at the effects of wars—including the arms races
that precede wars and the military downsizing that follows
them—tells us a great deal about the effects of government
spending. But are wars the only way to get at this question?

When it comes to big increases in government spending, the answer, unfortunately, is yes. Big spending pro-

grams rarely happen except in response to war or the threat thereof. However, big spending cuts sometimes happen for a different reason: because national policy makers are worried about large budget deficits and/or debts, and slash spending in an attempt to get their finances under control. So austerity, as well as war, gives us information on the effects of fiscal policy.

It's important, by the way, to look at the policy changes, not just at actual spending. Like taxes, spending in modern economies varies with the state of the economy, in ways that can produce spurious correlations; for example, U.S. spending on unemployment benefits has soared in recent years, even as the economy weakened, but the causation runs from unemployment to spending rather than the other way around. Assessing the effects of austerity therefore requires painstaking examination of the actual legislation used to implement that austerity.

Fortunately, researchers at the International Monetary Fund have done the legwork, identifying no fewer than 173 cases of fiscal austerity in advanced countries over the period between 1978 and 2009. And what they found was that austerity policies were followed by economic contraction and higher unemployment.

There's much, much more, but I hope this brief overview gives you a sense of what we know and how we know it. I hope in particular that when you read me, or Joseph Stiglitz, or Christina Romer, saying that cutting spending in the face of this depression will make it worse, and that temporary increases in spending could help us recover, you won't think, "Well, that's just his/her opinion." As Romer asserted in a recent speech about research into fiscal policy,

The evidence is stronger than it has ever been that fiscal policy matters—that fiscal stimulus helps the economy add jobs,
and that reducing the budget deficit lowers growth at least
in the near term. And yet, this evidence does not seem to be
getting through to the legislative process.

That's what we need to change.

ACKNOWLEDGMENTS

This book reflects the contributions of all the economists who have struggled to get through with the message that this depression can and should be quickly cured. In writing the manuscript, I relied, as always, on the insights of my wife, Robin Wells, and much help from Drake McFeely at Norton.

INDEX

Page numbers in *italics* refer to figures.